D0322740

## Africa Now

*Africa Now* is published by Zed Books in association with the internationally respected Nordic Africa Institute. Featuring high-quality, cutting-edge research from leading academics, the series addresses the big issues confronting Africa today. Accessible but in-depth, and wide-ranging in its scope, *Africa Now* engages with the critical political, economic, sociological and development debates affecting the continent, shedding new light on pressing concerns.

## Nordic Africa Institute

The Nordic Africa Institute (Nordiska Afrikainstitutet) is a centre for research, documentation and information on modern Africa. Based in Uppsala, Sweden, the Institute is dedicated to providing timely, critical and alternative research and analysis of Africa and to cooperation with African researchers. As a hub and a meeting place for a growing field of research and analysis, the Institute strives to put knowledge of African issues within reach for scholars, policy makers, politicians, media, students and the general public. The Institute is financed jointly by the Nordic countries (Denmark, Finland, Iceland, Norway and Sweden).

www.nai.uu.se

## Forthcoming titles

Margaret C. Lee, *Africa's World Markets*

Karuti Kanyinga, Duncan Okello and Anders Sjögren (eds), *Kenya: The Struggle for a New Constitutional Order*

Thiven Reddy, *South Africa: Beyond Apartheid and Liberal Democracy*

Anders Themner (ed.), *Warlord Democrats in Africa*

## Titles already published

Fantu Cheru and Cyril Obi (eds), *The Rise of China and India in Africa*

Ilda Lindell (ed.), *Africa's Informal Workers*

Iman Hashim and Dorte Thorsen, *Child Migration in Africa*

Prosper B. Matondi, Kjell Havnevik and Atakilte Beyene (eds), *Biofuels, Land Grabbing and Food Security in Africa*

Cyril Obi and Siri Aas Rustad (eds), *Oil and Insurgency in the Niger Delta*

Mats Utas (ed.), *African Conflicts and Informal Power*

Prosper B. Matondi, *Zimbabwe's Fast Track Land Reform*

Maria Eriksson Baaz and Maria Stern, *Sexual Violence as a Weapon of War?*

Fantu Cheru and Renu Modi (eds), *Agricultural Development and Food Security in Africa*

Amanda Hammar (ed.), *Displacement Economies in Africa*

## About the author

Mary Njeri Kinyanjui is a senior research fellow at the Institute for Development Studies, University of Nairobi, Kenya. She holds a PhD in geography from the University of Cambridge. She researches on economic justice, small businesses, economic informality, social institutions and issues of international development. She has published articles in the *International Journal of Entrepreneurship and Small Business*, *Hemispheres*, *African Studies Review*, *African Geographical Review* and *Journal of East African Research and Development*. She has been a visiting scholar at the International Development Centre (IDC) at the Open University in the UK and at the United Nations Research Institute for Social Development in Geneva. Some of her publications include 'Women informal garment traders in Taveta Road, Nairobi: from the margins to the center', *African Studies Review* 56(3): 147–64 (2013) and *Institutions of Hope: Ordinary people's market coordination and society organisation alternatives*, Nsemia Publishers (2012).

# Women and the Informal Economy in Urban Africa

From the Margins to the Centre

Mary Njeri Kinyanjui

Nordiska Afrikainstitutet
The Nordic Africa Institute

Zed Books
LONDON

*Women and the Informal Economy in Urban Africa: From the Margins to the Centre*
was first published in 2014 by Zed Books Ltd, 7 Cynthia Street, London N1 9JF.

www.zedbooks.co.uk

Copyright © Mary Njeri Kinyanjui 2014

The right of Mary Njeri Kinyanjui to be identified as the author of this work
has been asserted by her in accordance with the Copyright, Designs and
Patents Act 1988.

Typeset in Arnhem, Futura Heavy by Apex CoVantage. LLC
Index: rohan.indexing@gmail.com
Cover designed by Rogue Four Design
Printed and bound by

A catalogue record for this book is available from the British Library
Library of Congress Cataloging in Publication Data available

ISBN 978-1-78032-631-3 hb
ISBN 978-1-78032-630-6 pb

# Contents

# Acknowledgements

The fascination with the movement of women from the margins to the centre was prompted by a television commercial that showed a *mama mboga* (vegetable vendor) hawking vegetables in an Asian upmarket settlement in Nairobi. Rather than shouting herself hoarse to attract customers, as some traders do, she resorted to using a mobile phone to market her goods to customers. One of her customers was a female Asian in a nearby high-rise apartment. After the transaction, the customer used a rope to lower a bag to where the *mama mboga* was. The *mama mboga* then packed the vegetables into the bag and the Asian woman in turn pulled it up to her apartment.

This advertisement triggered a number of thoughts in me. First, I started thinking about the predicament women have been put in by masculine planning ideologies. One of the women is a hawker moving around with a basket on her back, calling out to customers to buy her goods, while the other, the client, is confined in an upmarket, high-rise building. The other implication of this commercial is the unchanging nature of women in the city as seen through the eyes of the television commercial developer. I personally identify with the predicament, having been born and bred in a village and having migrated to the city as a young adult. I came to Nairobi only when I joined Kenyatta University College in 1980. It is in this city that I have been searching for space and opportunity for the last 30 years.

Since I came to the city to pursue a university education, I have witnessed the constant struggle of women to move from the margins of socio-political and economic activities to the centre of the city. I witnessed the period when most shops in the city were either owned or run by men of Asian origin with African male shop assistants. There were very few women shop operators or owners. The majority of the women were either mobile hawkers or were situated in designated markets such as Kenyatta, Gikomba and Jericho. With time, this situation has changed. Women have moved into the central business district. Female faces are appearing behind the shop counters, while in some places, such as Taveta Road, women have taken over the entire street.

There are many people who have walked with me in my attempt to interrogate and understand the movement of women from the margins to the centre of the city whom I wish to acknowledge. First, I wish to thank my research assistants – Perpetual Njeri, Peter Twigg, Mathew Kimaru, Ruth Kimaru, Leila Nyaanga and Joseph Kabiru – for carrying out the survey interviews. Second, I wish to acknowledge Professor Ragnhild Overa, Inga-Britt, Professor Ilda Lindell, Professor Beth Maina, Philo Ikonya, Thiven Reddy, Birgitta Hellmark Lindgren, Sonja Johansson, Anniel Njoka, Joseph Kirika, Francis Kanyoni, Fredrick Mwangi, John Kiragu, Seneiya Kamotho, Josephat Juma, Esther Wanjiru Mburu, Pauline Wambua, Susan Wothaya, Lydiah Gitau and Dr Marjory Waweru for the roles they played in the different stages of the development of this manuscript. Third, I wish to recognize the participants at the following seminars in which I presented some of the findings and had interesting discussions: the British East African Institute, Nairobi; the Nordic Africa Institute; and the Department of Geography, University of Bergen. Fourth, I wish to acknowledge the Nordic Africa Institute for giving me a three-month fellowship to do part of the writing of the manuscript. Fifth, I am grateful to the women respondents who took time out of their busy schedules to give me an account of their socioeconomic activities and experiences in their quest to move from the margins to the centre. Sixth, I am grateful to my parents, brothers, sisters, nephews and nieces for cheering me up during the process of writing. Seventh, I cannot forget my friends Lydia Gitau, Angela Kamau, Anne Kamau, Felix Kiruthu, Wanjiru Gichuhi and Eunice Wanjoya for their support.

I also wish to thank my daughter Mercy Nyambura for buying me books on urbanization.

### Indeed Structured Living Indeed

The walls—look the same
The pictures on them tell it all.
The floor carpeted, as good as new;
Where are the holes in it ...
Or the patches filled with memories?

The way—a short distance
Yet the mileage is high,
The wear and tear minimal
Not from one, two or three
Many a people walk this hall

To and from the vantage point ...
They hobble back and forth,
Seeking solace, sharing affection.
Sometimes walk past
Or rain a series of questions—
Instructions!
Oblivious they run along

The hallway—a bees' hive—is spotless
The clean up after the keeper of house
No lint left behind ...
Back to the vantage point
Same questions,
Similar answers.
Back to the trail once more.
Maybe tomorrow they'll remember
Or the day after.
Even then, I will be waiting ...
I will be waiting at the vantage point.

# Economic informality (*jua kali*) spaces in Nairobi

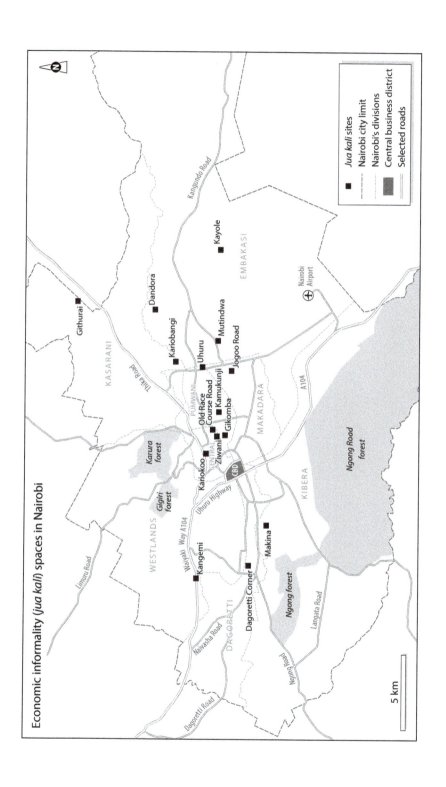

Legend:
- *Jua kali* sites
- Nairobi city limit
- Nairobi's divisions
- Central business district
- Selected roads

5 km

# 1 | Introduction

Urban analysts in the global South are concerned with the failure of African urbanization to resonate with the theories of urbanization. Countries in the global South are urbanizing at a very fast rate into what Davis (2004) calls 'a planet of slums'. Rather than a strong middle class evolving in the cities, a larger subaltern population is emerging that lives in slums and ekes out its livelihood in the informal economy (Beall et al. 2010; Simone 2001b). Urban planning theorists are therefore interrogating whether a metropolis that is based on subaltern urbanism can actually be formed.

Economic informality abounds in Africa. Its activities include hawking, market trade, craftsmanship, manufacturing and repairs. While economic informality provides livelihood and employment to a majority of the urban population, it has been a major source of conflict with modernity and order in the city. In southern Africa, for example, Kamete (2013a) documents how the cities in the region, faced with informality, have faced an uphill task in restoring order. In Nairobi, city authorities have for a long time struggled with the management of economic informality.

African cities have tried to address economic informality without understanding how it functions. Women constitute an important constituency of the urban population and the majority are in the informal economy. One cannot speak of the informal economy in Africa without thinking about women. Urban markets in Nairobi, Lagos and Accra are dominated by women, who are responsible for a massive trade in food and clothes. Any analysis of the role of women in African city dynamism is fairly limited and tends to treat women as victims (Potts 1995). The crucial question is whether women in economic informality have the agency to be a productive part of the urban dynamism that is taking place in contemporary African cities. Kinyanjui (2013) has demonstrated how women in economic informality have navigated the journey from the margins to the centre in Nairobi.

Cities are highly complex social, economic and physical systems, and the success of these systems depends on various actors, elements and forces. The dynamic dealings between people, place and economy can be mutually supportive and self-reinforcing. Addressing these relations effectively also requires an integrated approach that considers the ripple effects of each action on the other aspects of the situation. Using the case study of women in economic informality in Nairobi, on the one hand this book illustrates women's agency and how they are negotiating their way into the centre of the city to be part of the urban dynamism, and on the other it recounts how the city of Nairobi has struggled with economic informality over time and how economic informality has resisted removal and penetrated the central business district (CBD).

Two incidents prompted me to write this book: a YU mobile phone advert on television and a visit to Taveta Road in Nairobi's CBD in 2009. The YU commercial depicted two women transacting business in one of the gated communities in Nairobi. One of the women, an African *mama mboga* (greengrocer) had bought a new mobile phone and was using it to contact her Asian customer in a high-rise building. To receive the vegetables, the Asian lowered a bag towards the vegetable vendor using a rope. Undoubtedly, the two women are confined to specific spaces in the city but one physically crosses the boundary and is further aided by mobile phone technology to bridge the socioeconomic gap in pursuit of livelihood negotiation.

While on a window-shopping spree in Nairobi's CBD in 2009, I visited Taveta Road. I observed that the street no longer looked the way it had when I visited it in 1994 when I started working at the University of Nairobi, situated at the western end of the CBD. Most of the shops on Taveta Road had been subdivided into stalls or kiosks and the shops were no longer dominated by male Asian and African shop attendants. Women had taken over. I wondered how this had happened within a short time, given that women had been historically disadvantaged by patriarchal planning ideologies.

The advert and the visit triggered me to think about the state and the impact of African women in economic informality after two centuries of urbanization in Nairobi. I carried out a questionnaire survey of women in selected areas of Nairobi where economic informality thrives, including Gikomba, Kenyatta Market, Kamukunji, Uhuru Market, Githurai, Westlands Market, Kawangware and Taveta Road. I supplemented the information garnered from the survey with semi-structured interviews of 53 women along Nairobi's Taveta Road and I followed this up with in-depth interviews involving key informants and case histories of selected women in Taveta Road. My sole aim was to find out about the role of women in economic informality, what participation in economic informality meant to them, and the strategies that the women in question used to overcome the barriers created by planning ideologies and gender insensitivity.

This book is about the struggle of women in economic informality to leave the city margins and access the city centre, the planning and gender insensitivity of which largely excluded them. It uses the example of business activity along Taveta Road to illustrate how women who were restricted to the margins of the urban economy have infiltrated Nairobi's CBD and have introduced the African indigenous market system through mobility, solidarity, entrepreneurialism and

2

collective organization. The women are thus contributing to the complexity of the urban morphology, and, in order to do this, they have dealt with the African city reality, effects of planning ideologies, gender inequality and economic informality.

## The African city in reality and theory

Women encounter the reality of the African city as it is presented in both theory and practice in their everyday livelihood negotiation. Harris (1992: x) observes that cities in developing countries are characterized by vast squatter settlements, shanty towns, a poor supply of basic amenities, rapid environmental degradation, traffic jams, violence, crime and urban sprawl that eats into the countryside. Murray and Myers (2006: 1) observe that African city life has been reduced to a dystopian nightmare manifested by limited opportunities for formal employment, a lack of decent and affordable housing, failing and neglected infrastructure, the absence of social services, pauperization, criminality and increased inequalities. Due to these flaws, cities in Africa and the developing world are considered structurally irrelevant in the realm of world cities and attract hardly any global investment (Robinson 2002).

The rapid urbanization, dominant economic informality, gender inequality and unplanned nature of African cities make them different from cities in Europe, North America, Asia and the Middle East. According to UN-HABITAT (2006), Africa will experience the most rapid urban growth in the world until 2050. It is estimated that Africa's urban population will reach 742 million by 2030, up from 294 million in 2000. The projected 152 per cent increase in Africa's urban population will be fairly large compared with Asia's (94 per cent) and Latin America's (55 per cent); this rapid growth in population is attributable to rural–urban migration as well as to natural birth rates in cities.

The question of why the making of African cities is flawed has been the subject of debate among African urban theorists (Freund 2007; Mabogunje 1968, 1984; Macharia 1997; Mbembe and Nutall 2004; Murray and Myers 2006; Robinson 2002; Simone 2004; Watson 2002, 2009). In his seminal work on cities in Africa, Mabogunje (1968) demonstrated that Nigerian cities were not different from cities in Europe and attributed their problems to their parasitic nature and to over-urbanization, whereby cities were growing at a faster rate than the creation of jobs and the development of physical and social infrastructure. In his work on backwash urbanization (Mabogunje 1984), he argued that urbanization in sub-Saharan Africa is not based on economic development but is more the product of failed development policies in both cities and rural areas, with the failure of development in rural areas generating rural–urban migrants who flood the cities. This backwash urbanization has resulted in the peasantization of cities, whereby peasant migrants with rural origins dominate the cities and introduce peasant-type lifestyles and norms of survival. These peasant-type strategies are reflected in housing and in the city environment.

In an attempt to answer the question of the urban problematic, Macharia (1997) first attributes it to the informality of the African state, which hinders Western-educated planners from creating formal nation states and cities. According to him, the Kenyan state is based on a social structure permeated by networks that operate along familial, ethnic, friendship and overwhelmingly patrimonial lines that affect its performance (Macharia 1997: 105). Second, he links it to the prevailing strong social networks that lead to informal-sector dynamism. These networks attract more people into the city and determine entry, choice of sector and transfer of skills. As more people join economic informality, they contribute to the growth and expansion of the African city.

Using the case of Johannesburg, Mbembe and Nutall (2004) highlight the complexity of the city-making process in Africa. They urge urban scholars to desist from viewing Africa as a residual entity and to negate the predominant readings on Africa that emphasize difference. They argue that Johannesburg's history, architecture and capitalist formation reflected in the city's money economy, individuality, calculability and fortuitousness (Mbembe and Nutall 2004: 365) closely fit a metropolis as defined in classical urban theory. The city, however, has shortcomings, such as ugly agglomerations and insecurity (Mbembe and Nutall 2004: 367).

The African city should be seen through its complex history, culture and economy. It should also be understood by the way in which people have transformed it and how it has in turn changed them. While literature abounds that illustrates how urbanization and urban planning have victimized Africans by condemning them to slums, street trade and the informal sector (Brown 2006; Garland et al. 2007; Mitullah 2007), there is little in the way of literature to show how Africans have configured the city through their participation in economic informality, hence the quest of this book to examine the state and impact of women in economic informality in Nairobi city.

Freund (2007) attributes the problems in the evolution of African cities to the colonial origins of African cities, arguing that the urban dystopia in Africa accrues from the fact that a large majority of African populations were denied citizenship in the emergent cities. In Nairobi, for example, the whites who dominated the city council struggled constantly for the enforcement of pass laws, repatriation of vagrants, removal of informal housing wherever it was deemed inconvenient, and establishment of curfews and no-go areas for Africans (Freund 2007: 93). This made the African population straddlers, with one foot in the city and the other in the rural area, and as a result their participation in civic action and investment in the cities was greatly affected. However, there is significant investment and a large amount of civic engagement in African cities, particularly in economic informality: for example, 70 per cent of the population of Lusaka is dependent on the informal economy (Moser and Holland 1997). In Nairobi, 2.7 million people are engaged in the informal economy, according to the 2011 economic survey of the Kenya National Bureau of Statistics.

In addressing the evolution of cities, Robinson (2002) challenges the urban theory that categorizes cities as global cities, world cities or developing world cities. She proposes an urban theory that focuses on the ordinariness of cities in terms of their diversity, creativity, modernity and distinctiveness. This entails looking at cities in greater detail in terms of their spatiality, ideas, resources and practices drawn from a variety of places – not infinite but diverse – beyond their physical borders (Robinson 2002: 549). This is in line with the objective of this book, which urges the need to investigate the diversity and creativity within the African city in terms of the African indigenous market concept, solidarity entrepreneurialism, inclusion of women in urban planning, and collective organization as a method of organizing business spatially in the centre of the city. It also means including gender in the construction of urban theory.

## Urban planning

To a large extent, urban planning may be said to be gender blind. Women have had to deal with an urban planning ideology that does not include them. The failure of African planners to plan for economic informality means that they do not plan for women, who form the majority. Lack of urban planning in cities in the global South in general and in African cities in particular is a major problem; the urban sprawl that surrounds cities in Africa has defied urban planning. Informal settlements characterized by a mix of residential, economic and agricultural activities are dominant features in cities such as Nairobi, Kampala, Lagos and Dar es Salaam, where they pose significant planning challenges. In an attempt to come up with planning models in African cities, Watson (2002) proposes that planners should first seek to understand the social and political environment of the cities in which they are operating. She observes that, while the three normative planning models – communicative, multiculturalism and just city – have relevance to city planning in Africa, their application is affected by a dysfunctional civil society and a client-based relationship between state officials, politicians, political groupings and identity politics in African societies. This analysis suggests that planning an African city is a fairly complex phenomenon because of the inherent conditions existing in African societies. Further, Watson (2009) observes that:

> the planning systems were inherited from previous colonial governments or were adopted from northern contexts to suit particular local political and ideological ends. In most cases, these planning systems and approaches have remained unchanged over a long period of time even though the contexts in which they operate have changed significantly (Watson 2009: 2260).

The problem of planning cities in the global South is also echoed by Roy (2009), who argues that rational planning in India is undermined by informality and insurgence. Informality in India exists because land is managed informally without fixed purposes and without being mapped according to regulations or laws.

There are no clear guidelines about what is legal and illegal, legitimate and illegitimate, authorized and unauthorized (Roy 2009: 80). According to her, while informality is a key feature of planning, it creates territorialized flexibility and paralyses state development by rendering governance, justice and development impossible. Essentially, her analysis illustrates that an informal city is also an insurgent city and does not necessarily represent a just city because the policing of the arbitrary and fickle boundary between legal and illegal, formal and informal is not just the province of the state but also becomes the work of citizens, in this case insurgent citizens (Roy 2009: 85). She concludes that informality rather than failure of planning is responsible for the Indian urban crisis.

The planning systems in Harare (Zimbabwe) apply different measures in dealing with the spatial unruliness of the affluent and those in informality. In Operation Restore Order, illegal structures were destroyed and vagrants, street children and vendors violently relocated; however, illegal land users in affluent spaces were given a reprieve and time to regularize their properties (Kamete 2012: 67). It appears that sovereign and disciplinary power is exercised when the deviants are on the bottom rungs of society and hail from the less privileged parts of town, whereas more refined versions of disciplinary power are deployed when the offending parties are wealthier people in more affluent areas (Kamete 2012: 76). For effective planning, there is a need to reorient this kind of power-based planning whereby the sophisticated mode of pastoral power-based planning is extended to marginalized communities. This will facilitate their incorporation into orderly urban settings.

In a more recent paper, Kamete (2013b) argues that normalizing the informal sector by enforcing compliance with technical criteria such as health and safety, aesthetics and accessibility detaches the informal sector from economic and governance settings. He argues that planning standards that are generally considered normal are technical, and so the question of how to address informality has been removed from the realm of social, political and economic governance into the privileged realm of technical expertise (Kamete 2013b). This divorces informality from questions of social justice that are crucial to its existence: for example, how can women be incorporated into the urban economy if planning selectively destroys the informal economy where they abound?

Commenting on the planning of African cities, Miraftab (2009) calls for the decolonization of planners' city visions and images, emphasizing that the modernization pursued during the colonial period and perpetuated in the neoliberal era excludes some populations from the city. Using the case of South Africa's Western Cape Anti-Eviction Campaign, she demonstrates how insurgent planning is replacing hegemonic colonial planning regimes. The insurgent planning model aims to decolonize planning by taking a fresh look at subaltern cities and by understanding their uniqueness and values rather than seeing them in the light of planning prescriptions and fantasies of the West (Miraftab 2009: 45).

This book argues that de-westernizing or decolonizing planning theory is not enough: African aesthetics, architecture, philosophies, values and norms relating to the economy and space occupation should be introduced into the city. Women, who have been excluded from the planning realm for a long time, should be included. This means having a planning model that incorporates informality. This book documents women's struggle against urban planning ideologies, as they move from the margins to the centre, by drawing on their past cultural experiences and linking them with the present.

## Gender in the city

Gender inequality in African cities is a key concern in most of the analytical works (Chant 2013; Chen et al. 2004; COHRE 2008). Women are casualties of the urbanization process, which has offered them limited options to improve themselves. A majority of women in Nairobi still work in economic informality where they are handicapped by a lack of both information and start-up capital (Macharia 1997). Despite the women's work as traders, artisans and providers of assorted services, their activities are not captured in national government statistics: while the 2011 economic survey of the National Bureau of Statistics reports there are 2.7 million workers in the informal economy in Nairobi, it does not disaggregate the figures by gender. Moreover, women's issues in the city government are covered by the social services department rather than by key departments such as finance and planning. The social services department manages the city council markets, where most of the women conduct their businesses, and their market spaces are subordinated to those in the formal sector in terms of size of stall and supply infrastructure. The women are not provided with permanent leases for their stalls: after paying the stall rent, they are given a card that clearly indicates on the back that the city council can withdraw tenancy at any time. In addition, the markets lack flexibility in terms of time since they open at 6.00 am and close at 6.00 pm, which means that traders cannot operate night shifts.

Women's representation in central government as members of parliament, and in counties as county representatives, is considerably lower than that of men. The downplaying of women's work and insufficient representation in key decision-making bodies relegates women to subalternity and invisibility in cities. Women hardly ever appear in everyday print or electronic media, their voices being confined to special features in weekly or monthly magazines. Their stories, which are packaged in songs and dances, are not part of mainstream knowledge.

In terms of their physical location, the majority of women tend to be situated in peri-urban settings, informal settlements and city council markets. These are the least lucrative spaces in the city because they have limited economic activities. They are located in these spaces because of unemployment, lack of mobility and the constraints of low income, or because their spouses have low incomes. Women thus fail to enjoy the fruits of urbanization, unlike their male counterparts.

Indeed, according to reports from the United Nations Human Settlements Programme (UN-HABITAT), women in Africa's urban settings are marginalized because of their gender as well as because of physical and social conditions (UN-HABITAT 2006). The transformation of the African family in the face of urbanization has affected women most and has led to the creation of women-headed households in cities. These women-headed households are often poorer than male-headed ones.

Until recently, women's voices have been minimal in socio-political and economic discourse. However, this scenario is changing as women continue to assert themselves, demonstrate that they can measure up to duties that are performed by their male counterparts, are given a constitutional right to self-determination, and have their plight highlighted on the international scene.

The marginalization and invisibility of women notwithstanding, women in economic informality have been striving to overcome the confines imposed upon them by planning ideologies and patriarchy. They are doing this through mobility, solidarity entrepreneurialism and collective organization, and are thereby claiming positions in the city and contributing to the city-making process. For these women, feminism is not just about challenging male domination but acquiring space and opportunity for better living standards for themselves and their children. They are feminizing the city by sharing spaces, identifying livelihood opportunities and organizing collective action.

## Economic informality in the city

A large majority of women in cities engage in economic informality. Economic informality is an enigma in cities in Africa and has attracted a wide range of scholarship trying to operationalize and theorize it. Economic informality is assumed to be an economy of the poor where people who are unemployed, partially employed, casual labourers, street subsistence workers, street children and members of the underworld derive their livelihoods (Bayat 2000: 534). The International Labour Organization (ILO 1972: 5) describes the informal economy as petty traders, street hawkers, shoeshine boys and other underemployed groups on the streets of big towns, including both male and female wage earners and self-employed people. Moser (1978) defines the informal sector as the urban poor, which includes people living in the slums or squatter settlements found in the cities of developing countries. Five perspectives – dualist, structuralist, legalist, safe haven and heroic entrepreneurship – attempt to explain economic informality, which is seen as a product of poverty or marginalization in urban settings.

*The dualist perspective* The dualist approach is based on the works of Hart (1973) and the ILO (1972). These works propose that two sectors of the economy exist: the formal and the informal. The informal economy is characterized by ease of entry, reliance on indigenous resources, family ownership of enterprises, small-scale operations, labour intensiveness, adapted technologies, skills acquired outside the formal school system, and unregulated but competitive markets. The formal sector is characterized by difficulty of entry, frequent reliance on overseas resources, corporate ownership, large-scale operations, capital intensiveness, imported technology on a large scale, formally acquired skills, use of expatriates, and markets protected through tariffs, quotas and trade licences. Maloney (1999) argues that the presentation of dualism is inappropriate theoretically because unskilled workers can find jobs in both the formal and the informal sectors. Formal-sector jobs are likely to be undesirable because of labour protection taxes levied.

*The structuralist approach* Economic informality is also viewed as structural and closely linked to capitalism (Bromley 1978; Moser 1978). This approach critiques the dualist approach, argues that economic informality is a product of capitalism, and holds that the two sectors do not exist independently. An informal enterprise is dependent on large capital and provides subsidized goods to capitalist workers. Informality will exist only as long as large capital exists.

The informal economy in the dualist and structuralist models is positioned as being inferior to the formal sector and bent on survival rather than entrepreneurship. Using this viewpoint, it was argued that the informal sector would disappear in African economies once the survivalists' tendencies were catered for through modernization and formalization. Forty years down the line, however, the informal sector still survives in a majority of African economies. What was witnessed in the 1990s was the disappearance of the majority of import-substituting firms and government parastatals that constituted the formal sector, while export-led industrialization, the alternative strategy that was initiated to prop up the formal sector, has not been very successful as a strategy for development. In the same period, multinational corporations such as Coca-Cola adopted kiosks as part of their distributional frameworks, which meant that such firms recognized economic informality as a crucial dynamic in the distribution chain. This approach was also adopted by successful companies such as Safaricom, which integrated economic informality into its distribution model by sometimes using hawkers, as well as kiosks, to distribute its airtime credit cards. It also uses micro-retailers as agents for its monumental money transfer system M-Pesa. Equity Bank, which boasts 8 million customers, has cashed in on economic informality by situating banks in dominant economic informality spaces such as Gikomba, Kariobangi, Kawangware, Githurai, Kangemi and Ngara, to mention just a few. Other banks, such as Kenya Commercial Bank and Cooperative Bank, are also using micro-agents as distributors for their products in spaces of economic informality.

Large retailers who owned open-plan shops in Nairobi's CBD have been replaced by micro-retailers, some of whom are women (Ngwala 2011) who operate on principles of economic informality. Although the CBD was designated for formal retailers, the women have created their own terms by subdividing the shops into small cubicles or stalls. This phenomenon indicates that economic informality has survived and is resilient, despite the efforts to formalize it.

The fact that the formal sector is using principles of economic informality in its supply and distribution points illustrates the dynamism and special role that economic informality could play if it were given the same preferences that are awarded to formal firms. The formal sector should not be seen as the institution par excellence, with the informal sector a subsidiary (Kinyanjui 2011). The favoured position of the formal sector vis-à-vis economic informality has meant that the latter always has to fight for recognition in urban spaces (Macharia 2003).

*Legality* Hernando de Soto, the Peruvian economist, stimulated a different pattern of thinking when he published his work on Latin America's informal sector. According to de Soto (1989), the informal sector is a response to excessive regulation by the state. He argues that micro-entrepreneurs in the informal sector choose to operate informally with a view to circumventing the costs, time and effort of formal registration. De Soto notes that micro-entrepreneurs will continue to produce informally as long as respective governments negate free market principles and continue with processes that are cumbersome and costly in terms of bureaucratic red tape, and while there is a lack of property rights and difficulty in accessing productive resources such as finance and technology. In his view, unreasonable government meddling in factors of production is stifling private enterprise. De Soto champions the respect of property rights as a means of converting the informally held property of informal entrepreneurs into real capital (de Soto 1989). De Soto and his followers hail those who generate income for themselves and their families in the informal sector as the 'real revolutionaries', as they brave all manner of regulatory odds to be productive.

De Soto (1989) advocates the transformation of the 'class struggle into a struggle for popular initiative and entrepreneurship' and argues that the masses have united in a revolutionary front, not as proletarians against capitalist exploitation but as extra-legal micro-entrepreneurs against a bureaucratic state-directed economy that excludes them from becoming full capitalists themselves. Locked out of formal jobs and denied formal, legal title to their property, they have proceeded to create their own micro-enterprises and to institute their own set of occupation-specific extra-legal norms and regulations. He rightly observes that the informal sector has the potential not only to create wealth, reduce costs and democratize politics, but also to push out and replace the formal economy. Therefore, in comparison to other scholars who see informal economies of growth as exceptional, de Soto contends that the informal sector is filled with revolutionary potential.

De Soto (1989) argues that economic informality operates outside established laws and regulations because of the complexity of legal processes. There are many laws and regulations that economic informality entrepreneurs are required to abide by, and legislation is expensive and time-consuming for informal traders. They therefore choose to operate outside the law, with the result that informal operators are denied the rights that are accorded to businesses with formal legislation. He therefore recommends that laws and regulations that affect informality be eased.

Critics point out that, although the majority of policy makers for developing countries (i.e. the World Bank and International Monetary Fund – IMF) subscribe to this perspective, they neither offer practical solutions on how to incorporate 'the other path' into mainstream development nor do they possess evidence that proves that the informal economy can overcome the problems of a weak government apparatus under market liberalization (de Olarte 2001).

Larson (2002) refers to economic informality in *colonia* settlements along the United States and Mexico border as extra-legal rather than illegal. This is because informal businesses take place 'outside the structures of government regulation in particular labour, tax, health and safety, land use and environmental, civil rights and immigration laws' (Larson 2002: 140). She further observes that, viewed within the tradition of American social justice, informality contradicts both legality and equality and could be interpreted as an abuse of the law and a tolerance of exploitation and inequality. Arguing that the models of regulation used to maintain social justice in the American system contain unattainable standards that block the poor from providing for their basic needs, she concludes that there is a conflict of interest between legal ideals and informal realities.

The issue of informal-sector legality is a complex one. In the colonial setting, Africans were allowed to trade and to run businesses that would provide services for the African community. They were allowed to sell food, second-hand clothes, charcoal and wood and to carry out blacksmithing, to note just a few of the permitted activities. In the case of meat products, Africans were allowed to sell hooves, offal and intestines. The move behind legislating what was to be sold by Africans was spurred by the need to control and stop them from competing with the Asian and European merchant class. While African businesses were confined to African quarters, the bazaar and the CBD were the preserve of European and Asian merchants. Since it was not in the interest of the colonial government to promote an entrepreneurial African class, it thus ensured that Africans served as a reservoir of cheap labour for European and Asian businesses and farms.

In the 1950s, when the Mau Mau freedom struggle against the British colonial government began, the government started programmes for skilled training in trades such as carpentry and metalwork at Jeans School at Kabete. Women were organized into groups and taught arts, crafts and housekeeping. The colonial government also started issuing licences to a restricted number of people to sell tea, food, fruits and vegetables to the low-income workers working in the CBD and industrial area. Some vendors were also licensed to sell mushrooms, carvings and flowers to 'memsahibs' (or ladies) on street corners (Kenya National Archives 1973a). These vendors' licences were issued by the Provincial Commissioner, who was an officer of the central government and not part of the city council. In 1954, the city council took over responsibility for African welfare through the Department of African Affairs. By independence in 1963, the number of licensed hawkers was about 1,500.

The legality of the informal sector in Nairobi could be understood within the broader question of modernization and imperialistic control of African labour. The independent city government aimed to liberate the African from subordination in the workplace and other productive spaces. It also aimed to expand education, which would enable Africans to enter the world of modern commerce and business rather than dwell in the informal sector. Its legal ideals were therefore geared towards making Africans enter into formal-sector jobs. At the same time, the city authorities engaged in licensing economic informality for those who could not access entry into the formal sector, as will be seen later.

The legal ideals of self-governance and inclusion through licensing changed in the early 1970s. Hawking was considered a danger to the cleanliness of the city, as well as causing crowding and obstruction of pedestrian movement. While kiosks were supposed to be temporary, they had now become permanent. Hawkers also sold their goods near permanent shops and hotels, and residential quarters were turned into illegal beer halls, shops and restaurants (Kenya National Archives 1974). This implies that the issue of order, aesthetics and cleanliness prevailed over the principle of licensing and inclusion.

Of great concern were the issues of legality in terms of stock worth and the definition of sectoral activities to be licensed, such as household utilities. In the case of stock, hawkers with goods worth more than KSh (Kenyan shillings) 5, 000 required a trader's licence instead of a hawking one. However, because they were situated in temporary locations, they did not qualify for a trader's licence. This category of hawkers was accused of cheating the government. Activity relating to household utilities was vague because the goods were unlimited (Kenya National Archives 1978).

*Economic informality as a refuge or safe haven for victims of neoliberalism* In the context of global economic crises and restructuring, individuals who could not cope with the consequences of neoliberal austerity measures such as retrenchment from jobs, decline in incomes and removal of welfare were pushed into the informal economy. Bangura (1994) notes that austerity measures in

Nigeria forced the previously secure middle class into economic informality. Unni (2001) observes that the adoption of structural adjustment programmes forced women to join the informal sector while subcontracting for large firms offered opportunities to some women.

In Nairobi, economic informality is older than neoliberalism. Robertson (1997) demonstrates that women have been involved for a long time in the bean trade, which formed a type of economic informality business in Nairobi during colonial times. The bean trade struggled to survive in the context of agricultural imperialism during the colonial period, when maize, imported beans and English potatoes were introduced into the country. Neoliberal policies were introduced in Africa the 1980s by the World Bank and the IMF. They contained the structural adjustment programmes that comprised: the opening up of markets, cost sharing in hospitals and schools, privatization of government services, and retrenchment of workers in public and private services, as well as liberalization of exchange rates (Easterly 2005; Kraus 1991). According to Bangura (1994), these neoliberal policies resulted in massive job losses and the massive impoverishment of a large number of people who sought livelihoods in economic informality.

However, neoliberalism accentuated the entry of more people into economic informality since it was already a well-established mode of economic organization. Macharia (2003) observes that, by the 1980s and 1990s, people were moving from the formal economy and opting to establish enterprises in the informal economy, which had already become established. This is because 'the entrepreneurs in the informal economy gave it a new outlook and more people who could not join the formal sector felt comfortable joining the informal economy, popularly known as jua kali' (Macharia 2003: 25). The activities of these entrepreneurs made economic informality look attractive as an opportunity for alternative employment, and so the sector was recognized by citizens, governments and international donors as an alternative safety net from the effects of austerity and structural adjustment.

In 1985, President Daniel Arap Moi's visit to Kamukunji *jua kali* grounds prompted the creation of the Ministry of Research, Technical Training and Technology to spearhead the mainstreaming of economic informality, upgrade technology, ensure security of tenure of sites and organize economic informality workers into associations. Non-governmental organizations such as K-Rep, K-Map, the Small and Micro Enterprise Programme (SMEP) and Improve Your Business were supported by international donors who viewed economic informality as a safeguard for those people affected by structural adjustment programmes. These initiatives revolutionized the informal economy and labour market mentality to such an extent that most of the jobs being created in Kenya now are in the informal economy – in 2011, about 70 per cent of jobs created in Kenya were generated by the informal economy, according to the National Bureau of Statistics.

*Economic informality as revolutionary and heroic entrepreneurship* Economic informality should not just be seen in terms of dualism, structuralist, legalist or labour market dynamics, for it carries both revolutionary and dynamic entrepreneurship (Kinyanjui 2008a, 2010, 2011). Nijman (2010) and de Soto (1989) feel that economic informality is a revolutionary and heroic entrepreneurship since individuals engaged in it exhibit resilience and determination as they go about their everyday struggle to earn a living and improve their living standards. It is the path to urban socioeconomic dynamism for a large majority of people (Kinyanjui 2008b), since they derive their livelihoods, configure their identities and claim their space in the city from it. It also gives them the rubric for collective action and agency, which in turn serves as the nucleus for resistance to everyday subordination besides serving as a medium for participation and active citizenship.

The informal economy is deeply rooted in people's cultural practices, such as those relating to personal grooming (hair fashion, for example), indigenous food and entertainment (Kinyanjui 2010). Economic informality should be seen beyond the slum culture of helplessness and hopelessness for it drives action among the ordinary or subaltern populations (Nijman 2010). Economic informality is not an abnormal way of life but a people's creative response to the innate desire for survival and self-actualization.

Therefore, the disorder that comes with informality in the city is not a result of the sector being inherently disorderly but derives from the fact that planners have failed to come up with models to accommodate it. Illuminated by the available epistemologies of dualists, structuralists, legalists and labour market dynamics, planners have assumed that economic informality will disappear from the landscape of African cities. Unfortunately, this is unlikely to happen. As will be shown in later chapters, the informal economy will reinvent itself and encroach upon the CBD, as has happened in Nairobi, where open-plan shops have been subdivided into stalls and cubicles (Ngwala 2011).

Informality in cities in the global South has attracted significant scholarship. From a theoretical and policy point of view, informality is a problem that impacts on urbanization and the welfare of the people. It affects the formal order of urbanization in most of the cities in the global South (Roy 2005); it reflects the developmental nature of the cities in the global South that are characterized by underdevelopment, poverty, environmental degradation and disease (Robinson 2002). Yiftachel (2009) defines urban informality as the grey zone situated between whiteness and blackness, where whiteness represents legally approved safe spaces in the city and blackness is symbolic of the unsafe cities characterized by eviction, destruction and death. It is a product of urban apartheid that reflects the new colonial relationships. According to Roy (2005), urban informality is a mode of urbanization characterized by a system of logic and norms that govern the process of urban transformation. Informality is a product of state relationships that are based on exclusion and suppression of some forms of production.

From the above analysis, economic informality is a largely misrepresented and underestimated factor in urban growth. Women's participation in economic informality and the strategies they use to negotiate need further explanation. In this book, economic informality is defined as small-scale businesses that operate under the African indigenous market concept and that consist of a gathering of traders with strong social relations and associations based on friendship, kinship and ethnicity. It applies the principles of solidarity entrepreneurialism whereby traders reduce transaction costs by sharing space, transport costs and rents. The traders also offer each other financial support, as well as social insurance in the form of emotional and material support in times of crisis such as sickness and death.

The book is organized into nine chapters. Following this introduction, Chapters 2 and 3 provide a historical picture of the city of Nairobi and the relationship between the planners and economic informality. Chapter 4 documents the positioning of women in the city, and Chapter 5 discusses the role of women's mobility in economic informality, while Chapter 6 presents the characteristics of women in economic informality. Chapter 7 discusses the women's search for spatial justice, while Chapter 8 discusses women's collective organizations. The conclusions are presented in Chapter 9.

# 2 | Theorizing planning and economic informality in an African city

Cities all over the world are spatial manifestations of buildings for human habitation and production. They are the spaces where people live and work. They evolve over time and reflect the different socioeconomic waves of development and transformation that societies go through. Myers (2011) observes that African cities evolve in a peculiar manner that defies current theories and models of urban development in geography, sociology and planning. This chapter theorizes the planning of economic informality in Nairobi.

The question of the formation of contemporary cities in Africa has been addressed by many analysts, including Murray and Myers (2006), Robinson (2002, 2006), Freund (2007) and Myers (2011). The analysts agree that contemporary cities in Africa are fairly complex, are transforming, and are important sites of social, economic and political processes. The socioeconomic culture in the cities cannot be explained by a single paradigm. This is because 'cities in Africa are constantly changing, evolving, and mutating entities that resist efforts seeking to capture their essence, to categorize them in accordance with preestablished classification schemes, or to freeze them into rigid molds' (Murray and Myers 2006: xiii).

The process of making Nairobi was preceded by the building of an earlier settlement at Fort Smith in Dagoretti, where mostly the Gĩkũyũ community lives. The settlement relocated to the current location occupied by the railway station for security and gradient reasons in 1895. Nairobi was made a township in 1900, a municipality in 1928, and a city in 1950 (Kenya National Archives 1973a). Since then, the settlement has grown into a city with 3 million people, according to the 2009 population census.

The city is a hub of cultural, social, economic and architectural diversity, with buildings ranging from skyscrapers and shopping malls to mud houses and kiosks. Diversity is exhibited by the difference between companies such as Safaricom and Deloitte on the one hand, and, on the other, *mama mboga* (vegetable vendors) trooping with their bags of vegetables into the city neighbourhoods such as Parklands and Highridge.

Cultural diversity is reflected in the golf courses of Muthaiga and Windsor, the dusty fields where Mathare United Football Team plays, or the open spaces sometimes overflowing with sewerage where young children play *banya* (catch and throw ball) in poor neighbourhoods. Religious diversity is reflected in the Hindu temples, Muslim mosques and Christian churches, among others.

The spatial diversity is as contrasting as night and day. The shopping malls of Yaya, Sarit, Galleria, Thika Road Mall, Westgate and Village Market are completely different from shopping centres in Kariobangi, Soko Mjinga, Wakulima Market or Githurai. Residential houses in Mathare, Kibera, Korogocho, Kirimarigu, Mūkūrū kwa Njenga and Kawangware, for example, bear no comparison with gated apartments such as Wasini, Ainsworth and Tamarind that have recently been constructed in the upper-class neighbourhoods of Kileleshwa, Westlands and Lavington. The question is: why does the city present stark differences? Does the city formation follow a logical trajectory?

## The origin of Nairobi

The current position and state of informality of women in the city is a product of decisions made over a long time span. In order to understand the current state of affairs, there is a need to look at city making through a historical lens that will help in revealing how the anomalies and dystopia in Nairobi came about. In the case of women, it will also show that, for a long time, women have not been on the right side of a history that has privileged the trajectory of some to the centre. Instead, they have been struggling over time in economic informality to be part of the centre.

Apart from coastal cities in East Africa that owe their existence to the influence of the Arabs, most cities in the interior of East Africa owe their origin to contacts with the West. According to McCall (1955), new cities in most of Africa that served as administrative and commercial centres were the nexus between Africa and Europe. Like most cities in Africa, the city of Nairobi is a product of colonialism, owing its existence to the construction of the Kenya–Uganda railway.

The British, interested in the exploration of the rich and fertile plateaux of the Kenyan and Ugandan highlands, chose rail as their mode of transportation. In 1888, the Imperial British East Africa Company was granted a royal charter and exclusive rights to commercially exploit the African interior. The company spearheaded an ambitious campaign through the Kenya–Uganda Railway authority to build a metre-gauge, single-track railway line running from the Indian Ocean port of Mombasa into Kampala, Uganda. The groundwork for the line was carried out by Indian labourers dispatched from the British India protectorate.

As the rail work progressed into 1895, a small transport depot was established between the towns of Mombasa and Kisumu and was named Nairobi from the original Maasai name '*enkare nyirobi*', which means 'a place of cold waters'. The site was chosen for its adequate water supply, its elevated cooler grounds and the availability of ample level land for rail tracks, among other factors. When the rail head finally arrived in Nairobi in 1895, the town was made a shunting yard (a place where trains are shifted from one track to another) and a camping ground for the thousands of Indian labourers and other immigrant British colonial workers.

Initially, the railway station was supposed to be constructed at Fort Smith in Dagoretti, an idea that was shunned as a result of its unsuitable gradient, the high cost of maintaining the fort and the security risk posed by an antagonistic Agĩkũyũ community. Sir Gerald Portal, the agent of the Sultan of Zanzibar, reportedly described the company's station as being in a state of siege (the colony of Kenya was first administered from Zanzibar). He had to keep his scouts fully employed for fear of poisoned arrows or poisoned stakes set in the path of unwary travellers. Anyone wandering more than two hundred yards from Fort Smith would meet certain death (Kenya National Archives 1973a).

Nairobi was also developed as a counter-strategy to the effects of the German competition for African colonial territories. Captain Frederick Lugard, an administrator who played a major part in Britain's colonial history between 1888 and 1945, serving in East Africa, West Africa and Hong Kong, was interested in the relocation of the capital city of the Kenya colony from Mombasa to a more central location that was closer to the kingdom of Uganda for ease of administration. According to Captain Lugard, it was ideal that 'a government in order to be effective over so large an area and be capable of keeping in touch with the future outpost should be more central'. He also proposed that 'the government of East Africa ought ... to have its headquarters in the healthy and bracing uplands of Kikuyu or on the Mau plateau halfway between the kingdom of Uganda and the coast' (Kenya National Archives 1974).

Unlike European and North American cities that are hundreds of years old, Nairobi is therefore a relatively new city, since it was founded in 1899 as a railway terminal. It became a township in 1900, a municipality in 1928 and a city in 1950. Besides facilitating the occupation and administration of the British East African territory, Nairobi was established to serve the interests of imperialism; according to McCall (1955), the modern African town did not grow out of the need to serve its hinterland since its primary relationship was with Europe. The purpose of creating Nairobi was to facilitate the exploitation of resources in the White Highlands, given that it was strategically positioned in close proximity to the area, which was considered a 'great opportunity for European settlement'. The White Highlands were described by Frederic Holmwood, Sir John Kirk's assistant to the consul of Zanzibar, as:

a more charming region, which is probably not to be found in all Africa not even in Abyssinia. Undulating upland at a general elevation of 6,000 feet, varied and lovely scenery, forest crowned mountains, a land in fact where there was little to suggest the popular idea of the tropics (Smart 1950: 8).

## Economic implications of the founding of Nairobi

Nairobi city was thus founded as a holding ground for commodities such as coffee, sisal, wheat, animal products, wattle bark and tea extracted from the White Highlands and on transit to Mombasa for onward shipment to Europe. This had significant implications for the development of the city's economic base and social relations, since being a centre for goods in transit meant that the economic base was dependent on the metropole. The type of labour required was mainly low-skilled goods-handlers working in warehouses and in the railway station as loaders. This type of labour was unlikely to generate a high mass consumption society that would further generate industrialization in the city. Moreover, as a matter of policy, industrialization in the colony was discouraged because colonies were meant to serve as markets for manufactured goods.

The type of labour required also had an impact on the housing policy in the city, which demanded low-quality and cheap housing. Colonial policies did not encourage Africans to stay permanently in the city, instead encouraging only male labour migrants who would be housed in temporary settlements such as Majengo and Pumwani. The temporary situation of labour in the city and the low wages earned created a consumption pattern that depended on businesses that supplied goods in small quantities – this formed the genesis of the informal economy. For example, a bar of soap would be cut into small pieces and sold; cooking fat could also be subdivided into small quantities, as this was what the labourers could afford. Most of a labourer's wages consequently went into boosting the informal economy while the rest was transferred to the rural areas where the rest of the family lived.

At its inception, Nairobi began as a settlement for white and Asian immigrants: Africans were not part of the agenda in the formation of the city. Among the first immigrants was Sergeant George Ellis, who established a transport depot and built sheds for shops and posho (maize meal) mills. Other early settlers included the White Fathers of the Saint Austin Mission and Dr H. S. Boedeker, who became the township doctor. Some of the earliest Asian settlers included Dr Rosendo Ayres Ribeiro, Gyn Singh and Alidna Visram, who set up shops in the town centre (Kenya National Archives 1950).

The local government, which was initiated in 1900, was geared towards solving the problems of European and Asian settlers; the first meeting of the council was held on 12 July 1900 and consisted of two Europeans and two Asians. The meeting deliberated on seeking solutions for the eight problems that faced the city and that affected the two groups of people: the planning of a bazaar, street lighting, unplanned shops, lack of streets, lack of conservancy, lack of refuse collection, lack of police officers and lack of money.

The least tribal-conscious Africans were among the first migrants to move into the Nairobi settlement. The majority of them belonged to the Swahili community and were employed by the railway management to clear bushes along the railway line. Many upcountry people also moved into the settlement after the completion of the railway to seek incidental employment in railway maintenance. They lived on the fringes of the railway. Unemployment increased as more and more Africans moved into the area and the question of vagrancy in the city became an issue of concern. The township administration, citing its fear of rising crime (Kenya National Archives 1965b) as a result of the city's burgeoning unemployed population, requested the government to help control the African influx into the city. The municipal African Affairs Department was concerned that there were no strategies for dealing with the unemployable and criminal African cases. African housing was also inadequate as more and more Africans were moving into the city to live with the fortunate members of their family.

### The plight of Africans in Nairobi city

The separation of the urban population into Africans, Asians and Europeans and the adoption of different planning strategies for each group had significant effects on the way citizens related in the city (Kenya National Archives 1965a). To a large extent, the city was the preserve of the Europeans and the Asians. Since Africans were marginalized, there was no planning for their socioeconomic institutions. While Asians were allowed to build their structures (such as temples) in the city, Africans were denied such opportunities. Indeed, all the modernization and development strategies carried out by the missionaries and the colonial education policies encouraged Africans to discard their culture and adopt Western religion, architecture and consumption patterns. This explains why most of the urban architectural designs in Nairobi reflect Western or Asian cultural influence. Onyango (2010) bemoans the complete absence of African culture in Nairobi.

In Nairobi, some of the buildings that might attract the eye of an African who has never chanced to see New York, Paris or London include the Hilton Hotel, the Grand Regency (now Laico), the InterContinental, Serena Hotel, Safari Park Hotel and Casino, Kenyatta International Conference Centre and the Times Tower, as well as many more. None of these picturesque buildings depicts African culture or style, but it is common in former British colonies to see imitations of Western culture and technology and rarely to see progress in African culture (Onyango 2010: 65).

Moreover, since Africans were considered third-class citizens, their wages were kept low and as a consequence they could not afford the living standards in the city. Africans were assigned driving, cleaning and loading jobs, while some became shop assistants; these were basically low-wage jobs that had significant implications for the Africans' patterns of consumption and that could sustain only informal businesses. Africans were therefore not considered to be 'proper' citizens in the city, and so, when solutions for housing problems were being discussed, employers were urged to provide housing for employees rather than encourage them to own their own houses. Furthermore, the affairs of the Africans in the city were put under the jurisdiction of the African Affairs Department within the provincial administration rather than being the responsibility of the city department. Although the city was making attempts to include Africans in the city administration, it preferred to nominate a few Africans instead of having them elected by the population. With regard to the economy, Africans were encouraged to carry out craftwork or become hawkers in the city, supplying mushrooms, flowers and carvings.

Instead of allowing Africans to generate ideas and strategies for their well-being, the colonial administration decided what it perceived to be good for Africans to have and to do in the city. The African's entry into urbanization was regulated, while his participatory citizenship in the city was largely denied, and this had significant implications for the way in which Africans participated in the city's future. Thus, the issue affecting the populations of Nairobi is not only the fact that they are evolving outside capitalism, as stated by Roy (2011); rather, it relates to exclusion and denial of citizens' rights in the city. The post-independence African elites did little to break the defined paths of exclusion for a large majority of ordinary people. They adopted low-wage policies and the casualization of labour, a trend that ensured that the wages of most workers in the city were kept low and Africans' consumption patterns remained the same.

## The planning of economic informality in Nairobi

There have been attempts to plan Nairobi over time. Between 1895 and 1920, the planning of Nairobi was largely unguided and devoid of serious long-term thought. However, some semblance of serious planning was begun in 1926 when a number of controls on zoning were introduced. This was followed by the drawing up of a comprehensive plan in 1948 that laid down guidelines for development and earmarked land for residential, industrial and roadwork extension. In 1961, another plan was drawn up but it was abandoned because the country was about to receive its independence. In 1967, however, the need for comprehensive planning was mooted to address four main problems: housing shortage, water shortage, traffic congestion, and the rapidly mushrooming shanties.

*Growth and welfare: 1963 to 1983* This period was the heyday of post-independence Kenya. The city planners and general population were imbued with the spirit of self-governance and the desire to make Nairobi an African city. The ideals of self-governance comprised providing the residents with the space and opportunity to negotiate livelihoods, access health and acquire better education. It also meant the ability to move freely in the city without restriction. These ideals called for inclusive planning that involved making Africans part of the city. To meet the demands, the city adopted a growth and welfare approach that ran in tandem with the global welfare paradigm espoused by developed countries that were aiming to help developing countries emerge from underdevelopment.

The first African mayor in Nairobi, Charles Rubia, was particularly passionate about social and economic issues that affected the African population of the city. He paid attention to education, health, housing and economic opportunities for Africans. He was always at loggerheads with Asian councillors, European bureaucrats and the police administration because of their unfavourable stand on hawkers in the city. The city administration and the national government used a mix of policies to address the problems of economic informality, including hawkers' licensing, the African indigenous market concept, and *turudi mashambani* (the return to farms in rural areas).

HAWKERS' LICENSING Nairobi began thinking about economic informality soon after independence. The city was faced with a large African population that was largely unemployed, had low incomes and lacked proper housing. It was imperative that the African city administration tackle this inherited challenge by creating jobs for the African population as well as by allocating space for their activities. Mayor Charles Rubia vehemently fought for the unemployed population that had resorted to hawking and even threatened to resign if hawkers were not licensed. However, his Asian and European counterparts in the city administration resisted his advocacy.

Hawking as a mode of trade originated in the African indigenous market concept. African traders, especially women, were attracted into the new settlement to provide foodstuffs. Since no spaces had been allocated to the traders, they would move with their goods from one household to the next. As more people were drawn into the trade, household utensils, soap, oil, sweets, cigarettes and clothing were introduced. The demand for these goods was also increasing because of the growing number of Nairobi residents and people who came from upcountry to shop in the city. The hawkers' goods were cheaper than those in the shops because they were not subject to rent charges or other taxes imposed by the council. This made hawking a lucrative trade.

Hawking was tolerated because, at independence, the manufacturing industry was underdeveloped and could not cater for the growing number of migrants who were moving into the city after the relaxation of migration laws. Most jobless people, the majority of them being women, had little in the way of skills to enable them to be gainfully employed in the available jobs. They therefore resorted to self-employment as hawkers of household utensils, fruit, vegetables, cereals, fish and cooked food. The men especially engaged in the repair of vehicles, household goods and watches, while others were involved in metalwork and tailoring.

To deal with economic informality in the city, the first strategy that was employed was the licensing of informal businesses. A proposal was made that informal businesses should be granted licences, space to operate and a badge for identification. The informal businesses were allowed to trade in spaces where they would not compete with regular commercial shops or businesses but they were prohibited from putting up permanent structures – only grocery sellers were allowed to put up structures. The law required that businesses be operated by licensed individuals, and the employment of assistants or workers was prohibited by a city council by-law.

Licensing was carried out by the licensing superintendent together with the licensing committee. If denied a licence, one could appeal to the town clerk who would advise on the action to be taken. The licensing was procedural and had to be approved by the committee. It involved those seeking a licence sending an application to the licensing department specifying the type of activity they intended to carry out and the place where the business would be situated. The licensing department would shortlist the applicants and invite them for interview, and the committee would carry out a site visit to assess the location where the applicant intended to set up the business. If the site was suitable, the applicant would be issued with a licence and badge for a fee. The badge and licence had to be shown to the city inspectors as proof of identity and legality. The licensee could only trade in the activity specified at the site allocated. According to the plan, only 1,500 licences were to be issued to hawkers, but this number had risen to over 2,200 by 1973 (Table 2.1).

The logic behind the licensing was to regulate and control the entry of informal businesses into the city, control the total number of informal businesses, keep pedestrian pathways open, ensure a balance of services offered, ensure that only services essential to the common *mwananchi* (ordinary citizens) were licensed, control competition with licensed formal shops, and ensure that no criminal elements disguised as hawkers proliferated on the streets. The fee paid provided revenue to the council.

TABLE 2.1 Licensed hawkers, June 1973

| Activity | Number |
| --- | --- |
| Tea | 788 |
| *Irio* (mashed maize and beans) | 275 |
| Fruit and vegetables | 670 |
| Household utensils | 145 |
| Clothing | 266 |
| Handicrafts and curios | 45 |
| Flowers | 22 |
| Books | 11 |
| Other (eggs, snuffs, boxes, bottles, etc.) | 30 |
| *Total* | *2,252* |

*Source*: Kenya National Archives (1973b).

The fact that people in informal businesses applied for a licence demonstrated that they were law-abiding, which ran contrary to the perception that informal business operators such as hawkers were chaotic and bent on breaking existing laws and regulations. Hawkers were entrepreneurial: beyond their quest to earn a livelihood, they would identify a need and devise strategies to meet that need, if possible within existing rules. The letter below, which is addressed to the licensing superintendent and is from an entrepreneur applying to establish a food kiosk, illustrates that hawkers want to conform to city laws.

> Dear Sir,
> I kindly beg you to allow me to install the above kiosk in the area of the hospital. Major building construction work is being carried on by about 300 men to build hospital wards. I have seen how these workers find it hard to get their simple food for lunch. Many of them cannot afford feeding in the present hospital canteen because it is expensive for them. If you allow me, I shall cook for them simple food with less cost KSh 2 each meal. I shall also abide with the rules and conditions of health. Please help me. (James Karuri, 14/10/1975). (Kenya National Archives 1975b)

During the first ten years of independence, the process of licensing went well. However, the pressure of hawkers began to be felt in the city, with their numbers increasing to more than the licensed quota. This necessitated the carrying out of a survey to identify the true number of hawkers; the survey identified a total of 2,252 licensed hawkers and some 10,000 unlicensed hawkers. The unlicensed hawkers engaged in shoe-shining, vending newspapers, blacksmithing, bicycle and watch repair, selling *miraa* (khat) and operating barber shops, among other activities (Kenya National Archives 1978).

The council was in a dilemma because hawking provided jobs to people with limited chance of obtaining any other job and it was also a source of revenue for the council. Moreover, the hawkers had dependants. Thus, by driving hawkers out of business, their dependants, possibly entire families, would be affected. The council also acknowledged that hawking was sustaining urban livelihoods; for example, in Kariobangi, a moderately low-income settlement situated 10 kilometres from Nairobi's main employment centre, some 14 per cent of the labour force was self-employed. The monthly incomes averaged at KSh 900, and three-quarters of all household expenditure in the area on goods was made in the informal sector (Kenya National Archives 1976). According to the council, hawkers provided cheap goods to the people: fruit and vegetables were usually 50 per cent cheaper on hawkers' stalls compared with formal shops.

As hawkers began to entrench themselves in the city, they started setting up 'unsightly structures ... along streets and next to factories employing large numbers of low income workers'. Their kiosks were 'made of either plywood, carton papers or flattened tin walls with plastic paper or canvas' (Kenya National Archives 1976). The estimated 10,000 unlicensed hawkers created aesthetic and sanitary challenges in terms of the hawkers' disposal of waste water and refuse. The sanitary problem was accentuated by the outbreak of cholera in the city due to poor hygiene in eating places.

The hawkers formed a strong association to represent their interests. The strength of the association is reflected in its visit to then President Jomo Kenyatta at his Gatundu home on 14 July 1971 to request him to broker peace between them and the city council (Kenya National Archives 1972a). The hawkers' association held many meetings with the city council to discuss their plight in the city. They aired their opinion on forceful evictions, confiscation of goods and licensing. They also challenged the council to deal with unlicensed hawkers. Hawkers became a formidable force in the city.

The management and administration of hawkers in the city was characterized by several conflicts. Conflict between the council's inspectorate and hawkers increased, with the inspectorate accused of harassing and using undue force on the hawkers. There was also conflict between the licensing superintendent and the inspectorate department. The latter was accused of being punitive in the implementation of by-laws, destroying kiosks and shelters used by licensed hawkers who had been allowed to use them for a long time. The licensing superintendent feared that such clearances would cause disaffection among the general public and councillors (Kenya National Archives 1972b), while the hawkers resorted to demanding permanent spaces in the city.

There was confusion over the laws under which licensed hawkers were being charged in the magistrates' courts. Licensed hawkers would be charged under by-laws other than the hawkers' by-laws: for example, licensed hawkers who operated in kiosks, shelters or structures or who sold goods other than those shown on their licences would be charged under the food, shops and stalls by-laws of 1958, and under the eating house restaurants and snack by-laws of 1963. The law was vague because it stated that 'the hawkers should not operate at fixed places with kiosks, open structures and premises and that they should not operate in the open air and at no fixed places' (Kenya National Archives 1965b). The council was indeed contradicting itself because it was 'licensing people under certain by-laws and at the same time prosecuting them under different by-laws when they knew that the licences they have been issued with did not cover them' (Kenya National Archives 1965a).

There were conflicts between councillors and the non-elected workers that arose because councillors' positions and jobs depended on elections and were subject to the qualms of the electorate. If the electorate perceived that the councillors were underperforming and not representing their interests on the council, the councillors could easily lose their positions. Councillors thus opted to side with the people rather than with the city officers during the clearing of hawkers' kiosks and structures.

The hawker problem, the cholera threat and the fact that the hawkers were bold enough to visit the head of state forced the city authorities, the provincial administration and the office of the president to address the problem of hawking. Members of parliament in Nairobi, such as Mwangi Mathai of Langata, started lobbying for hawkers' rights in the city. At the same time, the International Labour Organization (ILO) completed its study on employment and equality in Nairobi and urged the government to acknowledge the role that the informal sector was playing in assuaging the problem of unemployment and inequality (Kenya National Archives 1975a).

Despite the change of heart among a section of city authorities, one town clerk, Mr J. P. Mbugua, described hawking as the 'most vexing problem in the urban scene throughout cities in most developing countries'. He felt that unless both the Nairobi city council and the Kenyan government adopted a more enlightened view towards hawkers and street vendors, the instability arising from social dissatisfaction would generate ugly political undertones in the future (Kenya National Archives 1975b). In another communication, the town clerk observed that the hawking problem was complicated by the social, political and economic developments that were taking place in the country. He intimated that:

> [problems] concerning hawkers always raise political overtones in various circles. It is always a very easy pastime to champion the cause of the underdog and quote instances of so-called inhumanity on the part of the officers even when those who criticize do not offer any solution to the problem. It is also easy for unscrupulous people to exploit the plight of the poor so as to achieve political eminence (Kenya National Archives 1962).

The provincial administration was also concerned about the unhygienic conditions of kiosks and the need to establish alternatives. The provincial commissioner challenged the permanent secretary in the Ministry of Health and the city council not to put this issue in 'cold storage' and highlighted the need to come up with reasonable kiosks (Kenya National Archives 1962).

The member of parliament Mwangi Mathai, in a letter to the mayor, Margaret Kenyatta, raised concerns relating to the way in which hawkers were being harassed on the grounds of the cholera threat (Kenya National Archives 1937–63). He asked the council to address the hawkers' security and could not fathom how a large number of Kenyans were being denied their human rights by being subjected to a life of fear and insecurity. He also requested that the council reconsider the by-law that prohibited hawkers from recruiting assistants or employees.

The permanent secretary in the office of the president, Mr Kareithi, asked the town clerk to carry out a survey of the economic informality workers. He also proposed that the government construct kiosks for the hawkers. It was agreed that donor funding should be obtained to carry out this endeavour, while the council would arrange the provision of land for the construction of the markets where such kiosks would be situated (Kenya National Archives 1973a).

THE AFRICAN INDIGENOUS MARKET CONCEPT  The master plan had designated the industrial area adjacent to the railway station and the central business district (CBD) as the main areas for business activities. These areas were largely designated for modern formal businesses that were adequately capitalized. The hawkers could not be situated in these two spaces: the only space available for them was Mwariro, located on the banks of the Nairobi River. It was called Mwariro (meaning 'where things are spread') because this is where the hawkers would spread their goods on the roadside while waiting for customers.

As part of the reforms initiated to address the hawkers' problems, the city council created a hawkers subcommittee that was charged with the responsibility of developing a policy for hawking in the city. One of the proposals made was to provide minimum basic services to people who were not hawkers but were engaged in other trades such as garage services in places including Shauri Moyo, Nile Road, Jogoo Road and Kariobangi. The provision of basic services would be financed using revenue collected from licences. It was also proposed that the informal traders be allocated land on semi-permanent terms. According to the town clerk, this would 'make them feel secure and enable them to improve their lot and stop feeling as outcasts' (Kenya National Archives 1962). He also recommended that the issuance of licences to poor people be accompanied by a far-reaching policy on hawkers that would secure their future and their economic life without endangering the general health of the population (Kenya National Archives 1973a).

To catapult Africans into business, the city adopted the African indigenous market concept as one way of getting Africans involved in economic activities. According to Mayor Rubia:

> the Government and the Council were in complete accord on the idea of
> providing Africans with economic opportunities, and were dedicated to open
> avenues in the economic field so that the existing racial imbalance was cor-
> rected (*Daily Nation* 1966).

To meet this demand, spaces in the city were allocated to host open-air African indigenous markets in Quarry Road, Jogoo Road and Kariokor. These open-air markets were situated close to the Eastlands, where a large majority of the unemployed Africans were living.

The regulations stipulated that the traders should come with their goods every morning and take them back home in the evening. The traders would also pay a market fee. No structures were supposed to be built in the open spaces.

However, since the traders were uncomfortable without shelter, they started constructing structures. This became a source of conflict between the council and the traders, and occasionally the council would come and destroy the structures on the grounds of poor hygiene.

The Cabinet Secretary was forced to look for funds to construct permanent structures in the market: for example, a fresh food wholesale market – Wakulima Market – was constructed at Mincing Street. Its construction began in 1965 and was completed in 1966. It consisted of new premises bounded by precast concrete walls, tarmac surfacing, water points and surface drainage. The shelves were built of reinforced concrete and stood at nearly two and a half feet above the ground (*Daily Nation* 1967a). Shopping centres for housing traders were also constructed in Ofafa, Jericho and Lumumba.

The construction of markets was not without its conflicts. Public health officers condemned them, a view that the town clerk and Mr Kareithi attributed to politics. Soon after their inception, the idea, as evidenced in the council's minutes, was to accommodate all licensed hawkers into the markets. As soon as a slight amount of coercion was used to get the licensed hawkers into the markets, there was a sharp reaction from some members of the council who had been lobbied by the licensed hawkers who did not want to be removed from the CBD. A resolution was passed that licensed hawkers be barred from these markets and several licensed hawkers left the markets (Kenya National Archives 1964–78).

One European official, Mr Kent, who opposed the idea of the market vehemently, argued that the council was losing money on the empty pitches while it was forced to allow anyone to move into the markets. The open-air markets proved to be a success because of the low overheads, but they were not a solution to the hawking problem. The three markets were upgraded but the venture proved expensive and they still did not accommodate all the traders, some of whom remained in the shanty markets outside. The costs charged by the renovated markets were also high for some of the traders. An alternative strategy for constructing markets was borrowed from Zambia and the council embarked on another round of building cheap markets that were of higher quality than the open-air markets.

The council also proposed that improved kiosks should be built for hawkers to replace the shanty kiosks that the hawkers themselves had constructed. This proposal was affected by a lack of finances and only a few were built in the city at a cost of £1,000 each. They were to be leased out at between KSh 400 and KSh 500 per year to the hawkers. These kiosks were more hygienic, were situated near clean water and had proper garbage collection.

THE RETURN TO FARMS IN RURAL AREAS (*TURUDI MASHAMBANI*) In the early days, Nairobi's planning philosophy was informed by the primate city concept.

The primate city is one that is supposedly two times larger than the next largest city in a country and has about a third of the national population. The *turudi mashambani* philosophy therefore endeavoured to control the growth of the population in the city by checking the movement of people into the city, especially those who could not be employed, through government decentralization and rural development policies. The paradigm focused on controlling the people instead of ensuring that the management of the city met the needs of the people already in the city. In a way, it curtailed urbanization nationally and condemned a section of the population to rural life.

To stop the influx of people into the city, the government initiated a policy of *turudi mashambani* (return to farms in rural areas). The policy aimed to control migration from the rural areas by initiating development projects: it was hoped that development in rural areas would lift the living standards in those areas and deter people from migrating into the city. The government set aside funding to improve rural agriculture, towns and infrastructure and to resettle the urban landless in rural areas. However, this project was not successful as people continued migrating into the city. The town clerk attributed this to the fact that people considered it easier and more lucrative to hawk in the city or sell illegally brewed alcohol rather than till their land.

## Conclusion

It is clear that the post-independence city council was ready to borrow from the traditional African market concept to solve its problem of hawking, and it is also clear that politics intervened to stop licensed hawkers occupying the spaces created for them. Perhaps the bottom-line question related to who was occupying the CBD. It was a political struggle that was yet to be won – the hawkers wanted a share of the CBD market. This conflict was taken into the new millennium when the open-plan shops were subdivided and occupied by micro-retailers.

Right from the beginning of the postcolonial city, hawkers' agency was demonstrated when they used all the measures at their disposal to resist whatever was contrary to their interests. They have a world view of what they consider to be just, right and proper: that is, accessing the most lucrative part of the city in order to engage in their livelihoods. It is not a dress rehearsal; it is a struggle for spatial justice that has entered the new millennium.

Some planners and legislators view hawkers as an important constituent of the city. For example, the former town clerk Mr J. P. Mbugua observed that hawkers were an important factor in urban life, and hence there was a need to address the urban problem. It was for this reason that the council authorities of the 1960s and 1970s attempted to plan for economic informality through licensing, the adoption of the African indigenous market concept, *turudi mashambani* and, finally, the policy of demolitions. Their efforts proved that economic informality cannot be wished away. It is entrenched in the city and is a way of deriving a livelihood.

Although the city administration laid down the foundations of economic informality as a metropolitan way of life, some factors stood in its way in the development of Nairobi as an inclusive city. In order to position the city in planning models, one must understand the sociology of the people involved. The makers of Nairobi included Europeans, Asians and Africans. The Europeans and Asians were considered permanent settlers in the city while the Africans were temporary residents who would return to their rural homes. The Europeans, who had previous experience of cities in the metropole, wanted to protect themselves from the savage Africans who would spread diseases (Freund 2007) and therefore created racially segregated spaces for the three races – European, Asian and African. The African settlements were further segregated on the basis of ethnicity; for example, the Gĩkũyũ were confined to Bahati while the Luo were confined to Kaloleni.

These spatial divisions generated mistrust and suspicion between races and tribes, undermining possible citywide social movements that could challenge and lobby for citywide policies. Each social category of people built networks around themselves, and these networks have been reproducing themselves in the urban sprawl of low-income spaces. For example, the Luhya dominate Kangemi and Kawangware; Kisii in Kasarani; Somali in Eastleigh; and Agĩkũyũ in Githurai, Zimmerman, Kahawa Wendani and Kahawa West. In some instances, spaces in the city are known on the basis of concentrations of different tribes, such as Kisumu Ndogo, or little Mogadishu.

The concentrations of different tribes in specific localities have a bearing on the leaders elected, with leaders of different ethnic groups being elected where their tribe is dominant. This further creates problems in the city administration hierarchy because representing tribal interests in city politics is not the same as representing class interests. Ethnic interests are linked to the home origin of the tribe rather than the city: when people mobilize along ethnic lines, they concentrate their development efforts in meeting the needs of their rural places of origin. For example, the leaders' strength lies in the formation of burial organizations for transporting bodies to rural homes; leaders in Nairobi will contribute money for funerals in rural homes so that their reputation is not affected; and they will support relatives and projects in rural homes to boost their image rather than mobilizing their tribes to own homes in Nairobi or supporting their small-scale businesses in the city. Arguably, this double citizenship in rural and urban areas results in divided loyalty in investments or civic engagement and affects people's behaviour in the city.

In the early days of Nairobi's development, the population was categorized into *athomi* (literate) and *acenji* (indigenous). The former were individuals who were educated, came to the city with skills and could easily be absorbed in formal-sector jobs in the civil service in government, in municipal jobs, hospitals, schools, industry, banks, insurance and administration.

The indigenous came into the city without skills, with little or no education, and were the majority. They came to the city to trade or to live with relatives who would start trading businesses for them. The indigenous were active in politics and had participated in the liberation struggle; they could not be wished away in the city's management or politics. The *athomi* did not take the Mau Mau oath because of their Christian background and level of modernization. Although the indigenous had played an important role in the liberation struggle, they could not take jobs in the formal sector because they were illiterate. However, they were aware of their rights. For this reason, when the hawkers paid a special visit to President Kenyatta, he could not ignore them.

The literate got jobs in the management of city affairs. They were the planners, engineers, surveyors and service providers. Unfortunately, these planners and managers did not have planning models for the traders because the European city model that they were emulating dealt with industrialists or owners of capital and workers. In this model, the owners of capital created jobs for the workers, and so the planners' role was to create spaces for the industrialists to establish industries and homes for their workers.

The ethos and world views governing the African indigenous market were largely absent in the planning models available to the African planner. This was the first challenge to the African planners and architects. While the literate were socialized with a culture of working for someone else, the indigenous did not have such a preparation. They were armed with desire, imagination and problem-solving skills based on working for oneself in solidarity with others. This disposition was informed by their culture and influenced their determination in livelihood negotiation, especially in self-employment.

Planning theory basically deals with a few owners of capital who can be easily planned for and workers who can be put in high-rise apartments in working-class neighbourhoods. In the Nairobi context, the planner was faced with individuals who had strong desires to negotiate their own livelihoods rather than work for someone else: working for someone else was associated with slavery, drudgery and oppression, and therefore freedom from working for someone else was one of the ideals of the liberation struggle. While the urban planner in the West is looking for owners of capital to create employment, the Nairobi planner is faced with the dilemma of planning for many individuals who want to create jobs for themselves.

Unlike the working class in European cities, whose welfare is dependent on the owners of capital – or the state when out of employment – traders in the African city are entirely dependent on themselves, their friends or kin for meeting their welfare needs. This reliance on self has implications with regard to what one does: it becomes a matter of life and death, especially in livelihood negotiation. This explains the persistence of the hawkers' struggles in the city. It is an attitude of 'I have got to do what I have to do until I am laid to rest. If I do not do it, I cannot eat.' There is no room for laxity. It means adapting and coping with changes in seasonality. It is not like the smooth order in formal employment.

The planner trained in the Western model of planning cities is not prepared for this. Traders would want to locate their businesses in places where they are assured maximum returns, even if those places are on the street. This generates conflict with the planner, who is trained to handle corporate interests. It is difficult to balance the interests of many traders, and the planners tend to locate these traders outside the CBD. Unfortunately, this becomes the source of conflict.

The urban planners faced a dilemma. Their training in modernization theory had taught them that everything traditional was backward and not fit for a modern city. But the indigenous people who had not been exposed to modernization were in the city and could not be wished away, since the elected government depended on them for legitimacy. Various values and ideologies were also at play in the city: African socialism and communitarian values versus individualism; growth and welfare versus the market; and concentrated capital versus distributive capital. As these values tried to get the upper hand in city planning and transformation, disharmony ensued. The challenge was how to strike a balance. Faced with all these conflicts, the town clerk observed:

> We have suffered from general lack of policy guidelines. Construction of markets for hawkers was said to be too elaborate and some were called white elephants. There is free land in our planning and we have been at loggerheads with some ministries with regard to development control. This is not usually welcome. Any developer would like to do what he likes. We insist on standards laid down, for example, on density of population, road thickness and drainage. In this respect we are unpopular (Kenya National Archives 1974).

The planning of the postcolonial Nairobi was difficult and problematic, and the Africans who took over the planning and management of the city experienced fundamental challenges. In one workshop on the management of large cities in Africa, the Nairobi town clerk reported that, although the city council had assigned some tasks to the city planners, there was a general lack of guidelines on policy, for example, on housing (Kenya National Archives 1973a).

Policy on kiosks and shanties oscillated between regulation and control on the one hand and freedom of occupation on the other. These mixed signals had a bearing on the kiosks and hawkers who could not invest in permanent structures because they knew that their positions were temporary. This negatively impacted on the way in which the kiosks were run. The great risks and uncertainties involved made the owners keep their businesses small.

While council authorities were encouraging the operation of kiosks on the one hand, they were curtailing their operation on the other. The Netherlands government at one time advanced the city council a soft loan of KSh 5 million to rehabilitate the kiosks on the Joseph Kang'ethe Estate and at the railway station. The mayor, speaking to a delegation of hawkers in his office, reportedly said that hawkers and vendors were important to the city. He challenged hawkers to maintain a high level of cleanliness and assured them that kiosks situated close to mains water pipes would be supplied with water (*Daily Nation* 1980).

This positive attitude towards kiosks changed as the first Organisation of African Unity (OAU) summit to be held in Kenya approached. The city was cleaned of shanties and kiosks because they were an eyesore and a symptom of the lack of modernization. On a fact-finding mission that the town clerk conducted on kiosks and shanties in Nairobi, he observed that there was uncontrolled growth in the number and size of kiosks, shanties and illegal hawkers' markets that needed to be curbed. The acting town clerk, M. M. Ombogo, told the *Daily Nation* that such structures would not be allowed to continue. Mr Ombogo said that the problem of illegal hawkers at Gikomba and Kamukunji needed serious consideration since stallholders in the council market were complaining that hawkers were usurping their business (*Daily Nation* 1981).

Whereas Charles Rubia had an image of a city that was inclusive, where both the low- and high-income earners had a roof over their heads, the succeeding city administrators seemed to care less about that; they were more concerned about beauty and cleanliness and how the city looked to the outsider rather than the quality of life of the people who lived and worked there. They did not plan for the people. They aimed to control the people and contain them so that they would not mess up the image of the city for outsiders. It is for this reason that a massive clearance of kiosks and shanties had to be carried out in preparation for the OAU summit in 1981.

Members of Kenya's elite, who were largely trained in Western institutions, imagine a city made of stone buildings with wide pavements, while the ordinary people, bred in the rural areas, imagine a city of temporary structures made of materials such as wood and corrugated iron sheets. It would be difficult to explain to some people why one should not put up an extension to the main house to serve as a kiosk or a rental building; why one should not sit under the bright sunlight in the open air to sell commodities on the street; or why one more person should not join the market and spread his or her goods out for sale to the public. The spatial manifestations of these worldviews, while generating community economies with collective institutions, also have other dimensions of overcrowding and an unregulated sprawl of enterprises. These spatial manifestations of the informal economy are found in Githurai, Gikomba, Kawangware, Wakulima, Dagoretti Corner, Mutindwa, Ngara, Kenyatta Market and Kamukunji.

The perception of who belongs to the city and who does not has been an underlying problem of planning in the city. In Nairobi, there is a subliminal feeling that there are *wananchi* (or citizens) and outsiders. The feeling is that the city belongs to the *wenye nchi* – that is, the modern, the clean, the orderly, those who have the financial clout and are connected, with a view to manipulating the running of the city – but it does not belong to the rest, who are ordinary and different. The perpetuation of the image of *wenye nchi* and outsiders in the city strongly influences the planning ideology.

Most of the people who engage in economic informality are viewed as outsiders who lack the city culture. They are thus allocated temporary spaces of occupation where they have no security of tenure; for a long time, they have been the subjects of eviction through urban cleansing policies. According to Muiruri (2010), violence against and eviction of hawkers is a violation of human rights and has a bearing on poverty levels.

Planning for economic informality is closely related to the African question and African identity in the city. It is also a class struggle between the elite and the subaltern. The elite are planned for in gated communities and suburbs that correspond to the former Asian and European parts of the city, while the subalterns are herded together in former African settlements. The planners have been slow to break this planning segregation. While shopping malls such as the Galleria in Langata are constructed for formal business, temporary buildings with no walls and with only makeshift roofs are constructed for economic informality businesses, as is the case in Muthurwa Market.

While Khayesi et al. (2010) state that there is a need to negotiate 'streets for all' where pedestrians, cyclists and street vendors would be catered for in transport policy and practice, this call should be made with the realization that people come to the city with different worldviews, and that these should be taken into account while planning. The city government's role is to balance these views and ensure that there is social justice in socioeconomic organization and in spatial manifestations. It would be wrong for one worldview to dominate the rest in planning at the expense of other perspectives. The informal sector, which largely reflects the ordinary people's mindset, needs to be brought into city planning either through a form of licensing or by the creation of markets, as was witnessed during Rubia's reign or as is happening in the design of the new Eastleigh shopping malls. The city administration's new-look kiosks, such as the ones in Roysambu and Harry Thuku Road, which are supposed to replace the old kiosk structures, are too small and get too hot during the day. As a consequence, vegetables and fruit spoil in the hot weather. The kiosks are also too few in number and therefore cannot meet the high demand. The design of the new Muthurwa hawkers' market is not suitable: it is too open. Perhaps an adaptation of the Eastleigh shopping malls might be a suitable model for accommodating the informal economy.

This historical analysis and discussion of the conflicts facing urban planners provides a different perspective to the available approaches to planning presented by de Soto (1989) and Roy (2005). De Soto (1989) views economic informality as a product of legal apartheid where the operators are denied property rights, while Roy (2005) views economic informality as an issue of exception from the state. However, in this instance, a young city government is struggling to address economic informality through licensing and the adoption of the African indigenous market on the one hand and to impose control mechanisms through *turudi mashambani* and demolitions on the other. The crux of the matter is the attempt to impose an imported city concept and ideology on a people with a different cultural experience. This model clashes with the resilient African indigenous market concept of sharing space and solidarity entrepreneurialism that is trying to put its imprint on the city.

# 3 | Economic informality in Nairobi between 1980 and 2010

## Introduction

In the previous chapter we illustrated how the city administration initiated the foundation of economic informality in Nairobi. This chapter documents the conflicts between the informal economy and the city governments that ruled between 1980 and 2010, a period that was characterized by a hostile attitude towards economic informality, with city governments bent on getting rid of it in their city.

The period between 1980 and 2010 saw an influx of many people into economic informality. This influx was occasioned by the increased migration that occurred due to deteriorating economic conditions and massive poverty in the rural areas; this in turn was caused by a decline in agricultural commodity prices. Most of these migrants sought livelihoods in economic informality. The World Bank and International Monetary Fund structural adjustment programmes, which had been initiated as palliative measures to arrest economic deterioration in African countries, worsened the economic conditions in those countries. The structural adjustment programmes comprised retrenchments in government services, the introduction of cost sharing in hospitals and schools, cuts in government expenditure, and liberalization of trade. The latter led to massive closures of import-substituting industries, which resulted in unemployment. The overall impact of structural adjustments forced many people to seek livelihoods in economic informality, and as the number of people in this sector increased in the city, they spilled onto the streets in search of spaces in which to carry out their trades. The escalating number of street traders caused significant conflicts with the city administration as they were perceived to be behind increased criminal activity and disorder in the city.

> We have in the City of Nairobi these days, hawkers with a difference; they are as confrontation-happy as they are prone to violence. No sooner are hawkers allocated sites on which to erect their kiosks in order to move them away from the up-market City Center, than other hawkers suddenly appear on City Center streets. No sooner are hawkers allocated plots on new sites other hawkers from God-knows-where surface at these sites and violence ensues. Then there are those hawkers in parts of the city who simply do not want to see

37

City Commission *askaris* [city police officers] and as soon as they spot them, a battle cry rings out and there is an all-out war of stones and sticks against batons and tear gas (*Daily Nation* 1990c).

The hawkers were also accused of offering unfair competition to genuine city taxpayers besides being a health risk because of their poor sanitation and hygiene habits.

> The fact that they provide a useful service and that they need to earn a living must be weighed against the danger to health they will pose unless their activities are restricted to the markets built for the purpose. It is obvious that the need to safeguard community health takes – or must take – precedence. This means that the by-laws must be enforced more vigorously (*Daily Nation* 1989).

## Management of hawkers

The ideals of integrating everyone in the urban modernity project seemed to lose ground by the 1980s and the decades that followed. In the 1980s, the council was replaced with a commission to manage the city. The commission withdrew hawkers' licences and, unlike in the previous decade when the pleas of operators in economic informality were at least listened to, the new regime was not responsive. According to the secretary general of the Kenya Street Traders and Nairobi Vegetable Association, Mr G. G. J. Githunguri, the city's 300,000 hawkers had their licences confiscated or denied renewal.

In another effort, the legal street traders held a meeting with the commission to protect themselves from the illegal ones. The chairman of the Kenya Street Traders and Nairobi Vegetable Association, Mr Maina, appealed to the council in a meeting at Kariokor Social Hall to protect them from illegal traders. He lamented that while legal hawkers were giving the council KSh 8 million in the form of revenue, they were not being given trading places in return. He showed them a licence belonging to a Ms Wambui Kibe that did not show her designated trading place, and he decried the eviction of traders from Jogoo Road without giving them an alternative space to trade in.

Rather than support people working in economic informality, the commission introduced rigid by-laws to control the hawkers and closed communication avenues between the hawkers and the city administration. They did this without consulting the hawkers' leadership. It was G. G. J. Githunguri's view that the officials of local authorities would change their attitude and hold a dialogue with the hawkers (Njihia 1985), but the commission went ahead and cancelled all licences issued to hawkers and banned them from operating in the central business district (CBD) (*Daily Nation* 1987). This ignited battles and demonstrations that saw one person die. The regular police had to be called in to quell the demonstrations.

During the hawkers' skirmishes with the city authorities, women were particularly disadvantaged. In a *Daily Nation* editorial, it was observed that women were 'arrested arbitrarily and forced to ride in City Commission trucks with children on their backs'. This, the reporter noted, was:

> a callous act of the *askaris*. The sight of hawkers laden with wares hurtling along the busy streets with baton-wielding City Commission *askaris* in hot pursuit powerfully resembles the frustration that Kenyans lived with in the colonial times. The symbolism becomes even more real when the women some carrying children on their backs are caught and roughly bundled into waiting vans and taken for an encounter with a magistrate (*Daily Nation* 1989).

Not everyone in government was happy with the way in which the city administration was handling the question of people operating in economic informality. The member of parliament for Kikuyu, Dr Njoroge Mungai, for example, appealed for rationality in handling the issue because both the commission and hawkers had legitimate claims. 'We want a clean city. Nobody, even hawkers, want to live in a dirty city,' he observed, 'but we should be human when dealing with this matter of city cleanliness' (*Daily Nation* 1987).

According to the Minister for Local Government, Professor Sam Ongeri, the hawkers' eviction would continue so that 'genuine rate payers in the Central Business District are protected to operate without interference' (*Daily Nation* 1998a). This incriminated hawkers by insinuating that they offered unfair competition and were not genuine taxpayers.

Some judges were sympathetic to the cause of the hawkers. For example, 'Lady Justice Joyce Alouch asked the Nairobi City Commission to pay damages of KShs 183,000 to a hawker whose goods and licences were destroyed by the city *askaris*' (Opanga 1989). This judgment was a clear indication that the hawkers have rights and that they can resort to justice instead of engaging in running battles with the *askaris*. One legislator, George Anyona, said that harassing hawkers was a national scandal and called for the resignation of the government and commission authorities concerned.

The city commission, however, continued with its anti-hawker stance. Dr Njoroge Mungai, the Kenya African National Union (KANU) chairman, criticized Mr Fred Gumo for demolitions of kiosks that were the source of livelihoods for ordinary people (*Daily Nation* 1990a). The commission's policies against ordinary poor people were also demonstrated by the demolition of Mworoto village on 25 May 1990. The callousness of the event was illustrated by the fact that Mr Fred Gumo paraded the city council *askaris* who carried out the operation before the press to counter a report by the provost of St Andrew's Church that some *askaris* had died or had been injured in the operation (*Daily Nation* 1990b). When the member of parliament for the area asked the commission to take responsibility for the action and resign, he was called a neo-colonialist and sacked from Moi's government. The then Minister for Local Government supported the demolition, saying that Mworoto was a den of thieves. On 6 July 1990, city council *askaris* invaded Gikomba Market and paralysed business operations. The *askaris* damaged business stands and rounded up many hawkers into waiting trucks (Mwangi 1990).

The operations of the city commission largely reflected the elite's arrogance and blindness to the plight of ordinary people as a result of their political power and privileges. It was a case of 'us, the moral' versus 'them, the immoral', or they are 'a den of thieves', as MP William Ole Ntimama referred to them. The ethnicized politics within the city commission and the government's vengeance against a Agĩkũyũ-dominated hawking business also had a bearing on the handling of people operating in economic informality. If the problem of hawking was solved and favourable conditions implemented, it would have benefited the Agĩkũyũ, who comprised the majority of people in economic informality.

The handling of people in economic informality in the 1990s was also affected by the relationship between the city government and the central government. Since the city administration was run by individuals affiliated to the parties in opposition, most of the people in economic informality were labelled a security risk and harassed by the central government. For example, all the MPs who opposed the demolition of Westlands Market – namely Paul Muite, Waithaka Mwangi and Charity Ngilu – belonged to the Social Democratic Party, while Maina Kamanda, the member of parliament for Starehe, belonged to the Democratic Party; both of these were opposition parties (*Daily Nation* 1998b).

While the hawkers were agitating for economic freedom and spatial justice in the city, the government was entrenching its political control and silencing the opposition from the grassroots. The government was keen to keep the opposition from infiltrating the volatile groups of hawkers by spreading them way out of the city centre and dividing them into smaller groups. If they remained in the city, the hawkers would spread disaffection with the city administration to other city residents and form a formidable force in the city centre. Political control of the emerging proletariat took centre stage, rather than the excuse of keeping the city clean. If the hawkers became economically powerful, they would threaten the existing power hegemony in the city. This perhaps explains why the city administration and the government were not willing to enter into dialogue with the hawkers.

The new millennium ushered in the multiparty government. Ideally, it was supposed to be an all-inclusive government that catered for the rich and the poor alike. However, in spite of the optimism among the informal economy operators that their plight would be addressed, the response towards hawkers was ruthless. A special police squad was formed to keep them out of the streets.

However, hawking in the city intensified, triggered by the high number of school and college graduates who were unemployed. Many of the hawkers in the streets went to school but could not get jobs because they were not connected to anyone (Mulwa 2009). Lack of social protection was said to be another reason why people went into hawking. 'We cannot compare our country with developed countries ... these are countries where the jobless are given free housing and a stipend' (Mulwa 2009).

Other factors that contributed to increased hawking in the city included: failure of the economy to produce quality and dependable jobs; sub-zero economic growth; the collapse of industries; and a cost-cutting mania in blue-chip employment (*Daily Nation* 2002). Lack of coordination between the Ministry of Local Government and the Ministry of Trade also led to an increase in hawking; since trade was contributing about 20 per cent to the gross domestic product, the two ministries needed to work together so that they could come up with suitable sites for traders, otherwise traders were left on their own to search for trading sites (*Daily Nation* 2006b).

In the 2000s, there was a widespread fear of subalterns taking over the city on the part of the established elite traders who were barely surviving due to the effects of structural adjustment. The need to protect the established traders led to another wave of battles between the regular police, city *askaris* and administration police. The hawkers responded by recruiting gangs to protect them from the police, while some allegedly acquired guns, machetes and petrol bombs for self-defence. On 5 July 2006, it was reported that hawkers had organized gangs that were strategically placed to protect their wares: it was not the hawkers themselves who would attack the *askaris*, but well-organized gangs hired for such a purpose (*Daily Nation* 2006a). The hawkers also reportedly raised money to prepare for counterattacks. Unlike in the Jomo Kenyatta era, when workers in economic informality could visit the head of state, the new millennium offered hawkers scant or non-existent access to State House. Although the hawkers put up stiff resistance in order to remain in the CBD and high-income neighbourhoods, they were overpowered and, to this day, only a few dare to venture there.

In the 1990s, Nairobi experienced intense criminal activity, which led to the city being branded as 'Nairobbery'. Business people were the main targets of crime, with thieves stealing from and killing their victims. The period was characterized by widespread fear, political unrest and insecurity. Over the decades following independence, Asians had steadfastly built their businesses and increased their assets as a community. Other businessmen perceived the development of the Asian community to be at the expense of their African counterparts, and when the clamour for constitutional reforms reached fever pitch, most Asian families were casualties as they were seen as favouring the status quo. Their families were robbed at gunpoint or killed and their shops were looted during the annual fracas that took place in memory of the 'Saba Saba' riots, despite the fact that a majority of them were third-generation Asians whose families had been in Kenya since pre-independence days. As one report in the *Daily Nation* (7 August 1993) put it:

A mystery gang gunned down four Asians in Nairobi on Thursday night killing a man and his wife and wounding a third man ... Neighbours said the gunmen left leaflets signed 'Sons of Liberty' warning Asians to leave Kenya. The attackers, whose number was unknown, fled after pouncing on Mr N. V. Jethwa, who has a business on Kimathi Street, his wife, Manju, and two relatives, Mr Shantilal Parmar and his wife, Chanda, [who] arrived at the Jethwas' house on Ngoa Road, Parklands, when they returned home from a night out.

Many Asian business people were thus forced to leave the CBD and to move to gated communities in the suburbs as they were often the targets of rampant robbery. As the Asian crisis was taking place, a man by the name of Nelson Kajuma introduced a new concept in the city for managing activities of economic informality. He would hire out empty spaces in the city from the council and subdivide them into stalls or kiosks, which he would let out to workers in economic informality. Economic informality workers who traded in these stalls were not harassed by the city council and they learned that they could trade in such shared spaces. Some hawkers picked up the concept and started looking for buildings where they could rent spaces – one of the buildings the hawkers occupied was the former Sunbeam market on Moi Avenue. Other hawkers looked for lodges in the city where they rented out rooms in groups. This phenomenon created a demand for stalls, and many landlords in the CBD started converting their open-plan shops, which the Asians were leaving, into stalls and kiosks. Women who already had collective organizations easily moved into these new spaces. Due to their solidarity, a woman who obtained a stall would invite her friends to join her in the building. The subdivision of open-plan shops created the space and the opportunity for women to gain entry into the CBD after a long struggle, as will be shown in the next chapter.

# 4 | Women in Nairobi

Cities in Africa are increasingly becoming feminized in demographic terms. There are about 1.5 million women who live in Nairobi and most of them live in conditions of informality. Table 4.1 below shows the distribution of the population of women and men in Nairobi between 1948 and 2009. The migration of women into Nairobi increased with independence: between 1969 and 1979, the female population of Nairobi grew by 69 per cent; between 1979 and 1989 it grew by 64 per cent; between 1989 and 1999, by 73 per cent; and between 1999 and 2009, the female population grew by 55 per cent. This indicates that the population of women has been growing and women are becoming an important constituency in the city.

In terms of distribution within the city, the 2009 census (Table 4.2) revealed that in Nairobi East and Westlands, the differences between the populations of men and women were very small. Nairobi East comprises the oldest settlement for Africans while Westlands mainly consists of high-income areas of the city. The distribution of the proportion of men and women in Nairobi West and Nairobi North differs by 2.3 and 2.7 percentage points respectively. Nairobi North comprises part of the central business district (CBD) and emerging unplanned

TABLE 4.1  Nairobi's population by gender, 1948–2009

| Year | Men | Percent- age of total | Women | Percent- age of total | Change (%) | Total |
|------|-----|----------|-------|----------|--------|-------|
| 2009 | 1,605,230 | 51.2 | 1,533,139 | 48.8 | 54.9 | 3,138,369 |
| 1999 | 1,153,828 | 53.9 | 989,426 | 46.1 | 72.9 | 2,143,254 |
| 1989 | 752,597 | 56.9 | 571,973 | 43.1 | 64.2 | 1,324,570 |
| 1979 | 479,448 | 58.0 | 348,327 | 42.0 | 69.0 | 827,775 |
| 1969 | 303,219 | 59.6 | 206,067 | 40.4 | 69.0 | 509,286 |
| 1962 | 190,606 | 71.4 | 76,189 | 28.5 | 170.4 | 266,795 |
| 1948 | 94,755 | 79.6 | 24,221 | 20.4 | 214.5 | 118,976 |

*Source*: Population census, Kenya National Bureau of Statistics, various years.

TABLE 4.2 Distribution of population by gender in Nairobi, 2009

|  | Male | % | Female | % | Total |
|---|---|---|---|---|---|
| Nairobi West | 352,227 | 51.2 | 332,538 | 48.9 | 684,765 |
| Nairobi East | 582,554 | 50.9 | 561,862 | 49.1 | 1,144,416 |
| Nairobi North | 545,701 | 51.3 | 516,385 | 48.6 | 1,062,086 |
| Westlands | 124,748 | 50.4 | 122,354 | 49.5 | 247,102 |

*Source*: Kenya National Bureau of Statistics, 2010.

TABLE 4.3 Highest level of education of population aged three years and above by sex in Nairobi, 2009

| Level of education | Male | Percentage | Female | Percentage | Total |
|---|---|---|---|---|---|
| Never attended | 73,986 | 45.5 | 88,518 | 54.5 | 162,504 |
| Pre-primary | 81,613 | 50.2 | 80,907 | 49.8 | 162,520 |
| Primary | 520,044 | 48.4 | 553,989 | 51.6 | 1,074,033 |
| Secondary | 510,609 | 54.1 | 433,539 | 45.9 | 944,148 |
| Tertiary | 141,787 | 49.3 | 145,862 | 50.7 | 287,649 |
| University | 110,946 | 57.7 | 81,391 | 42.3 | 192,337 |
| Youth polytechnic | 12,997 | 59.6 | 8,806 | 40.4 | 21,803 |
| Basic literacy | 4,115 | 49.6 | 4,185 | 50.4 | 8,300 |
| Madrassa | 4,437 | 48.9 | 4,628 | 51.1 | 9,065 |
| *Total* | 1,460,534 | 51.0 | 1,401,825 | 49.0 | 2,862,359 |

*Source*: Population census, 2009.

settlements, but the area also has many middle-income neighbourhoods. This implies that women are fairly well distributed in most parts of the city, although the tendency is that there are more men than women in most localities. The differences between men and women come in terms of education, employment and income.

In terms of education, Table 4.3 shows marked differences in education levels between men and women in 2009. Women have comparatively lower education levels than men: the percentage of women who had attained a secondary school level of education was 45.9 per cent, while for men it was 54.1 per cent. The difference between men (57.7 per cent) and women (42.3 per cent) with a university education was more glaring. Women reported the highest proportion (54.5 per cent) of individuals without any formal education; this compares with men at 45.5 per cent. Women with no formal education had to seek assistance when transacting business. Since urban incomes are closely linked to education levels, it logically follows that women's incomes are lower than those of men. Similarly, due to their low levels of education, women are more likely to derive their livelihood from the sprawling informal economy than men.

### The position of women in the city

Although women's presence in the city has improved, there are questions with regard to their quality of life there (Chant 2013; Chant and Pedwell 2008; Chen et al. 2004). In Nairobi, women informal traders have been confined to the margins of the city in slums and peri-urban locations. Prior to the new millennium, women in business in Nairobi city tended to be hawkers who sold fruit and vegetables or an assortment of clothing. Other women were confined within markets such as Gikomba, Jericho, Uhuru, Kenyatta and Kariokor, which were far out of the city centre and close to low-income residential areas. Together with male hawkers, women risked removal from the streets by the city police in their attempt to keep the city clean, modern and secure. In the 1980s and 1990s, it was common to see women running away from the police with children strapped on their backs and their goods scattered all around. There were very few women trading in the city centre in regular shops: the CBD was a masculine space dominated by Asian businessmen and African male shop assistants. The lack of female dominance in the city is reflected in the small number of women who are councillors in the city administration. They are also underrepresented in the Nairobi Central Business District Association – this is a new organization that is supposed to work with the city council in managing city affairs as well as representing business interests.

Women are important in both production and reproduction spaces. In production spaces, a good number of women are engaged in small-scale manufacturing and trade, mainly in the informal sector. They also work in factories, offices, hotels or households. Women's role in reproduction entails renewing the labour force through birth and the nurturing of young ones. Thus, they contribute to the growth and expansion of contemporary cities.

In spite of the important role that women play in the cities, the majority are confined within the subaltern category of the urban population. Due to their numbers and to unfavourable policies for women's urbanization, they comprise the less dominant groups, they are largely invisible, and they do not participate in active citizenship in the city. They are largely unemployed, disadvantaged and more likely to suffer from poverty and violence than their male counterparts in the city. Further, as they are not considered within the city planning agenda in Nairobi, women's issues are confined to the social services division of the council. There is a general assumption that the production and reproduction roles of women naturally fit into cities. This assumption holds that the city is accommodating to both men and women equally. Feminists would disagree with this perspective. Turshen (2010) observes that capitalism, the engine of production in the city, exploits women's production and reproduction roles. Women are often the most underpaid workers in factories or are concentrated in low-paying jobs such as teaching and nursing.

While urbanization is perceived to be a transformative process that can change the lifestyle and livelihood of people in the global South according to Boserup (1970), who calls for women to be urbanized so that they can achieve equality with men, Thorbek (1988) contests this perspective using case studies drawn from Ratmalana in Colombo (Sri Lanka), Khlong Toey in Bangkok, and Thailand. She argues that women become part of slum cultures where gender gaps in material conditions are immense.

*Factors explaining women's position in the city* According to Macharia (1997) and Mbiti (1969), women's migration was controlled by masculine colonial policies that favoured male migration and a patriarchy that ensured their domination and control by men. Historically, women were disadvantaged in terms of migration. They were forced to migrate because of unhappy marriages, conception out of wedlock or arranged marriages. They were usually unskilled and could not naturally fit into city jobs. They moved from their disadvantaged position into the urban environment where they were pushed into subalternity. They lost control over their labour on farms and over their bodies, as was prescribed in traditional ways of life.

Policies and patriarchy locked women out of urban and capitalist enterprises (Sheldon 1996; Robertson 1996). While colonial policies encouraged the migration of male labourers to work on farms and in mines, factories and shops, women were forbidden by law to migrate from rural areas to the city. According to Sheldon, women were not only restricted from migrating into the cities but also faced challenges in getting waged employment, and so their entry into the urban working class was much slower than that for men.

Barnes (1992) documents how the colonial government in conjunction with male workers controlled women's mobility out of the fear that it would lead to the breakdown of family order, which was crucial to sustain the supply of labour. While on the one hand the colonialists discouraged family unions among male labourers but encouraged prostitution so that the men would not be distracted by family responsibilities, on the other hand they discouraged single women from moving into the city for fear that they would become prostitutes and transmit venereal diseases. This was also another way of annihilating African society by destroying the family unit, which formed its basis. However, through prostitution, some women who were free from the surveillance of their parents or male relatives gained a livelihood in the city and joined the city's circuits of capital (Bujra 1975).

Further, the colonial government also engaged in the marginalization of women's interests. The colonial government provided housing for male workers, which mainly consisted of single rooms with limited amenities. However, this does not mean that conditions in the colonial city were easier for men. Men were required to carry identity passes in the city; if found without them, they could be arrested.

Apart from colonial restrictions, African society also frowned upon women migrating to the city. Robertson (1996) has documented the efforts to control the movement of Agĩkũyũ women into the city. Women who migrated into the city denounced the patriarchal authority of their fathers and husbands, and there was a general feeling that single women who migrated into the city were prostitutes. There was therefore a concerted effort by the elders to control the movement of women into the city (Robertson 1996). Similar efforts by elders to control the migration of women are also reported for Luo women. Okuro (2006) illustrates how the Ramogi African Welfare Association worked with the colonial government to repatriate women from towns to rural areas for allegedly causing harm to society. The women would have their hair cut, be dressed in 'gunny bags' (burlap sacks) and walked through the street in an endeavour to shame them before they were repatriated (Okuro 2006: 71). The colonial government supported the elders' efforts by carrying out swoops on women in the city and repatriating them to the rural areas.

Popular music such as the song '*Cumi cumi i nguo cianyu nguhi*' ('Short short dresses, miniskirts') admonished women migrants. In this song, the singer questioned what women migrants in miniskirts were going to do in Nairobi if not prostitution. '*Cehura cehura*' ('Strip strip'), another popular song, discouraged women from migrating into the city by warning them that they would be stripped by men 'like loaves of bread'. Such songs extensively demonized women migrants, stigmatized them and warned them against migrating to Nairobi city. Both the colonial government and African cultural institutions participated in discouraging women's migration, but for different reasons.

While the increase in women's migration to the city was accompanied by a demand for urban space and opportunity, there were no official policies to support women migrants. Women were seen as part of a family whose issues would be handled by the male spouse. The only issue relating to women that seemed to bother the city council authorities in the early days was single motherhood; it was proposed that a hostel for single mothers be built at Jamaa and managed by Catholic nuns of the Sisters of Charity. It was not until 1979 that women were issued with identity cards. The lack of identity cards had denied women the chance to transact business in banks or to own land. In addition, in 1968, parliament passed the Vagrancy and Prostitution Act that allowed policemen to arrest women suspected of being prostitutes or vagrants.

Apart from the Government Secretarial Training College, teacher training and nursing courses, there were no institutions that trained women with limited education for the world of work in industry or the retail trade. Women's advancement was left to the Maendeleo ya Wanawake organization, which was supposed to teach them modern housekeeping skills, arts and craft. Government or city council involvement in the welfare and general advancement of women (especially those with limited education) was minimal. The women were left to fend for themselves in the informal economy.

A review of the Nairobi City Council Hawker Licence file for 1973 to 1975 (RN/1/169) reveals letters from women who were making desperate requests to the town clerk to be issued with hawker licences in the city. Their quest to be hawkers was prompted by their inordinate desire to fend for their family, by their lack of employment and by low educational levels. The hawker licence would not only enable them to trade in the city without harassment, but it would also make them less dependent on their male spouses and make them active citizens in the city.

However, a licence did not provide automatic security for women traders in the city. The women were still vulnerable victims of male security personnel and faced regular harassment from city council *askaris*, as is evident in the case of a woman who is reported in Hawker Licence file RN/7/8/14. The woman protested to the licensing superintendent by returning her licence and abandoning her four children at the superintendent's office. The licensing superintendent issued the licence to someone else and took the children to the police station. This single case is a testament to women's desperation in the city. A licence was not enough to secure and regularize their position as traders and urban citizens. This woman's resistance is symbolic of the everyday encounters that women faced in the streets: during the day, they would be harassed as hawkers; at night, they were subject to the Vagrancy and Prostitution Act of 1968.

Another letter, dated 14 April 1971, illustrates how women were terrorized in the city even if they were licensed to do business. The city council *askaris*, who were most often men, were brutal towards women and would scatter the women's goods and arrest them. The women lacked security in both the city and the household: in the private space, men left them with children to fend for, while in the public space the male *askaris* denied them their rights to negotiate a livelihood in order to feed their children. The women would be arrested either for hawking or for loitering with immoral intentions according to the 1968 Prostitution and Vagrancy Act. Their genuine desire to participate in legal livelihood strategies encountered setbacks, and to all practical purposes women were second-class citizens in the city.

The cultural dislocation of women from their traditional rural homes made women's adjustment to city life difficult. In the rural set-up, a woman's life was programmed according to her lifecycle: for example, among the Agīkūyū, a female underwent stages that determined her reproductive and productive roles. These stages included the *kairītu* (girl), when she took care of babies. This stage was followed by the *karīgu* (teenager), when she was ready for initiation and would accompany her mother to the farm, where she learned to be an adult *mūirītu* (or unmarried adult woman) – *mūirītu* is the stage after initiation when a woman prepares for marriage. After marriage, the next stage was *mūtumia* (married woman). This was also the childbearing stage. During this stage, the woman was given a piece of land by her husband to grow food crops and she also engaged in periodic retail trade. This was the stage when a woman was actively engaged in reproduction and production in the household and in the public domain. The last stage in a woman's lifecycle was the *nyakīnyua* (elderly woman). A woman at this stage was past childbearing but she took care of grandchildren and also worked on her farm. During this stage, a woman could be conferred with an elder's title and she could participate in religious ceremonies as an elder.

Since reproduction and production responsibilities were defined by these stages, migration into the city upset the progression of the woman's lifecycle. Upon migration, the *mūirītu* stage was prolonged, since often a husband was not forthcoming in the city. Courtship spaces such as dances where young men and women used to meet in the rural areas did not exist in the city, and most of the male migrants had their wives in rural areas. With delayed marriage and difficulty in finding a husband, the *mūirītu* in the city would decide to start having children. This in turn gave rise to single parenthood or female-headed households in the city, and single parenthood entrenched the need for women to engage in livelihoods. Single women with or without children were a problem that both the colonial and the postcolonial city had to deal with, as we shall see later.

The migration of women into the city also meant the loss of the farm where they used to work and produce food crops, which they periodically sold in markets. Alienated from their familiar environment, they were largely considered as idlers or delinquents. The only available jobs for unskilled women involved the provision of domestic services to male workers and middle-class families. Their choices for participating in business were limited because trading was controlled by the city authorities (Robertson 1997).

Women were also confined to subalternity because, unlike the men, they lacked a rural base that could serve as a safety net. Without this rural base, women relied solely on their livelihood activities in the city and were therefore more prone to material deprivation than their male counterparts, who had both a moral and a material support base in the rural area that cushioned their subsistence in the city. To a large extent, the men were able to cope with low urban wages because of the support they received from these rural areas. They could reinvest the money earned in rural production, hence enhancing their survival. The women's predicament was made worse by the fact that some of them had left the rural areas to escape forced marriages. Women therefore entered the city in a disadvantaged position.

The discrimination against women in the city was legally sanctioned by the Prostitution and Vagrancy Act of 1968. The act was introduced by the Minister for Home Affairs, Mr Robert Matano, and seconded by the Attorney General, Mr Charles Njonjo. The justification used for the introduction of this act was that crime, beggars and prostitutes had increased in the city. Mr Njonjo argued that ladies of the night masqueraded in the towns, with the intention of obtaining money through evil means. The bill, if passed, would therefore give the government the power to round up these women, who were considered a 'disgrace' to the country, and repatriate them to their homes so that they could help their parents till the land.

Although the bill was passed, it encountered opposition. The MP for Kisumu Rural, Tom Okelo-Odongo, observed that the bill was similar to the South African law that required Africans during the apartheid era to carry passes. He further stated that women would be discriminated against under the new law. The bill empowered a police officer to arrest anybody he suspected of crime, begging or prostitution (*Daily Nation* 1974). The bill had far-reaching consequences on the spaces women accessed and led to heightened anxiety over how they dressed in public. This was especially true for the women in the informal economy. It was at the discretion of any police officer to determine whether a woman was a prostitute based solely on subjective observation. The new law therefore also controlled the mobility of women in the city.

It appears that the male-dominated parliament was not ready to pass bills in favour of women. A majority of parliamentarians perceived women as opportunists and mercenaries out to exploit men. In opposing Elijah Mwangale's motion on the Children and Young Persons Act, which sought support for children born out of wedlock, Joseph Martin Shikuku alleged that some women were claiming support for a child from as many as five men who did not even know the woman concerned (*Daily Nation* 1967b). Rather than pass a law to support unmarried mothers after the abolition of the Affiliation Act, which forced men to take care of children born out of wedlock, the authorities preferred to keep the women in institutions such as Jamaa House in Eastlands (Munene 1972). These institutions were inadequate and also poorly funded.

Unmarried but expectant women were subjected to a lot of pressure. They were treated as outcasts in society; they rarely received support from the fathers of their children; they were kicked out of jobs and schools; and they were rejected by parents and friends. While the presidency directed that the sacking of pregnant girls from employment and the labelling of children born out of wedlock as illegitimate be stopped, there were no remedial policies for subaltern women who were out of employment, deserted by husbands or widowed. The majority of these subaltern women had no choice but to seek livelihoods in the informal economy as hawkers, micro-traders and garment makers

Generally, the planning ideology did not have long-standing strategies for incorporating women into the urban modernity project. In the colonial mindset, women should have remained in the rural areas and should only have paid visits to their husbands in the city. Most of the responsibility for engaging women in the modernity project was left to women's organizations such as the League of Women, Young Women's Christian Association and Maendeleo ya Wanawake. These associations later embarked on programmes that looked into the welfare of unskilled and unemployed women in the city, including programmes that involved the establishment of home industries for women to train women in home economics and general hygiene.

In addition to the generally patriarchal attitude to women found in the formulated official policies, women did not have formal identification documents until 1979 when they were issued with identity cards. This meant that prior to this year they could not conduct businesses that demanded that the individual possess an identity card. They had to have a male relative to proffer an identity card on their behalf. It was also difficult to transact business with banks, where women needed to know a staff member in order to be assisted. Without an identification document, women could not buy land and always had to be cautious in case they were arrested by the police and charged with loitering with immoral intention. Women, therefore, could only engage in informal transactions.

There was a generally negative attitude towards women migrants. Women who migrated as wives were under the control of their husbands. In patriarchal family settings, a woman had to seek permission from her husband to secure employment or start a business. She could not even use her income freely as she was obligated to pool it within the family setting. A married woman without a job stayed in the city at her husband's discretion and the husband could decide to repatriate her back to the rural area at any time. The woman was therefore subordinated both at household and at state level and confined to spaces with limited circuits of capital, power and commodities. These spaces were usually in slums and informal settlements. It was in these spaces that they engaged in production and reproduction and supplemented the husband's income by engaging in the informal economy. As women retirees also found their way into the informal economy, it became a refuge for a majority of women.

Women were also treated as intruders and were not accorded the dignity and respect that came with formal jobs. According to Bett (1967), many people in Kenya do not respect women even if they hold a high level of responsibility in the country. Bett (1967) urges the Kenyan population to treat women equally because marginalizing them will stagnate the country's socio-political and economic growth. In a debate on whether married women should work, one person observed that, had he been a member of parliament, he would have voted against married women working because by working and being married they ended up being jacks of all trades but masters of none.

> One wonders why they [women] ever decided to be married at all. If you think you are too tired to look after your appearance, too tired to pay sufficient attention to your husband, too tired to make your house worth living in, too tired to prepare a meal worthy of its name, too tired to control your temper, too tired to direct your housemaid, then we could as well add 'too tired to be a successful young wife'. Therefore, I would advise you to resign (Muhavi 1969).

Hostile sentiments towards women taking up jobs in the public domain were also expressed by Ng'alwa (1970). He stated that it surprised him that the inflow of women into offices was increasing tremendously. This increase meant that men were being barred from employment opportunities. According to Ng'alwa (1970): 'One obvious problem with women is that their productivity is low – first, because it is natural and, secondly, because they rarely exert the maximum effort.' He further challenged the idea of women's rights by stating that the nation was not going to feed on women's rights: 'We want enough bread and butter for the whole society not to see resources used for metamorphosing women to become whites' (Ng'alwa 1970).

The structural adjustment programmes initiated by the World Bank and the International Monetary Fund (IMF) affected the positioning of women in the city. Gacheri (1995) observes that during the economic decline of the 1980s, women suffered a great deal partly due to the IMF- and World Bank-initiated structural adjustment programmes, which spurred lay-offs and unemployment in the formal sector. Moreover, cronyism, nepotism and extreme corruption meant that even those employed hit a glass ceiling because promotions were not meritorious. Instead, they were dished out to politically connected individuals. In addition, the agricultural sector that had supported rural employment in coffee, cotton and pyrethrum production was collapsing. This led to massive rural–urban migration and involvement in economic informality. Women were not spared. They had to derive livelihoods in the informal sector locally known as *jua kali*. The Minister for Culture and Social Services, Mrs Nyiva Mwenda, decried the way structural adjustment programmes had relegated women to suffering. Supported by Attorney General Mr Amos Wako, she was particularly concerned about the increased drop-out rate of girls from schools (*Daily Nation* 1996).

Essentially, urbanization has deteriorated conditions for women and feminized poverty for a majority of women. Indeed, women are involved in a 'gender struggle' that entails concerns for children, husbands, mothers, friends and relatives and constitutes the bridge between material conditions and social relationships (Thorbek 1988). These social relationships are part of the social infrastructures through which action takes place in contemporary cities in Africa (Simone 2010). Through the social infrastructure, women are incorporated into the circuits of capital, power and commodity in the city.

Reproduction roles are not compensated or facilitated in the majority of African cities. In Nairobi in particular, there is no government-subsidized day-care facility to help release women from reproductive duties so that they can engage in other productive responsibilities outside the home. Moreover, kindergarten education for ages three to five has to be paid for – and existing day-care facilities are very expensive – while primary education for youngsters aged six to 14 is free. This means that up to the age of five, when the child is most in need of love and nurturing, it is the responsibility of the mother to cope with the demands of both work and home, without subsidy from the government.

All these factors combined – including dislocation, lack of rural support, regulation and control by masculine policy planners, lack of jobs and skills – subjected women to subalternity. Thus, incorporating women in the urban modernity project by providing them with gainful employment and livelihoods, easing their responsibilities in domestic spheres and providing skills should have been part of the ideals of self-governance in the postcolonial city. This positioning of women in the city can be traced to colonialism and the early days of urbanization, when women were forced to participate in circuits of labour and capital situated in the less dominant spaces of the city, in informal urban forms, on the streets or outside the CBD.

## Women's struggle for ascendancy: the 1960s to the 1980s

Postcolonial developing world feminists (Mohanty 1988; Spivak 1988) decry the failure of women in the global South to transform the masculine culture and the concomitant Western domination. According to Spivak (1988), subaltern women do not speak because they are victims of domination both by their culture and by the West, which tries to rescue them from their marginalized position. Mohanty (1988) argues that the voices and experiences of developing world women have been appropriated by the hegemonic white women's movement. She further states that women in the developing world are presented as a homogeneous category based on sociological unity that is determined by their role in domestic and primary production. Further, the women are presented as objects – powerless, poor, uneducated and sexually controlled.

In African feminism, the perspective of low-income women, women from the grassroots, or women operating in economic informality is often not heard. These categories of women are written about by elite women and men in academic institutions and non-governmental organizations. It is assumed that elite feminists who have gone through the process of modernization and have received a Western education have the sole right to speak for other categories of women (Beoku-Betts and Njambi 2005). Indeed, according to Basu (1995: 10), many middle-class women's movements have failed to mobilize poor women, assuming that class interests can be subordinated to gender interests. It is therefore least expected that the woman in economic informality will act or speak for herself or articulate her rights in any way. She has to be spoken for and made aware of her rights. Works on women in economic informality are viewed through modernization and developmental paradigms that tend to ignore women's agency in the struggle against male domination and material deprivation (Karanja 1996; Ngau and Keino 1996; Tsikata 2009). In these analytical frameworks, the woman is a victim and is overwhelmed by the economic informality in which she works (Mitullah 2003; Muiruri 2010).

Women in economic informality are concerned with economic survival rather than with challenging male domination. Their participation in economic informality is a struggle against material deprivation that has come about because of patriarchy and planning policies. One of the ways in which women reclaim themselves from material deprivation is through trade (Robertson 1997); these women's efforts are in line with Mikell's (1997) perspective that African feminism is concerned with 'bread and butter', culture and power issues. In Nairobi, women are concerned with getting the space and opportunity required to negotiate livelihoods so that they can attain food security, educate their children and secure shelter. Women in economic informality draw on their cultural experiences to acquire space and opportunity in a city that is dominated by a masculine planning ideology. This kind of feminist struggle by women in economic informality is not often highlighted in feminist discourse, and it is for this reason that Mugo (2012) calls for redress for the absence of ordinary women in the literature.

While African feminists such as Diallo (2003) have aggressively condemned practices such as polygamy, female genital mutilation, forced early marriages and domestic violence, they have ignored the role of the subaltern woman in participatory citizenship. Subaltern women have participated actively in the bean trade (Robertson 1997) and in rice market chains (Kinyanjui 2008b) in Kenya, while women garment traders have survived the onslaught of neoliberalism in Uhuru Market (Kinyanjui 2003). Despite their low levels of education, their domestic responsibilities and marital status, they have exhibited some degree of control in the informal economic sphere.

The feminist discourse's omission of women in economic informality is not accidental: Kenya's development planning in the colonial and postcolonial eras has hardly addressed the social order that privileges male and female elite workers as opposed to subaltern workers. Kinyanjui (1999: 267) observes that policy documents subtly and consistently undermine female roles and expectations through omissions and assumptions. The benefits of Kenya's new constitution, which was inaugurated in August 2010 and is being hailed as gender friendly, are yet to be realized.

In view of the above, Nnaemeka (2003) appeals for a 'nego-feminism', a type of feminism that is goal-oriented, cautious, accommodating, adaptable, open to diverse views and that engages African issues. The critical question is how does African feminism, which is largely taught in women's studies and gender departments or as African studies in universities, reach the terrains of subaltern women in the informal economy? Can subaltern women in cities lay claim to African feminism as their path out of marginalization?

African feminism should not relegate women in economic informality to 'problems that need to be solved' but should portray them as people who are capable of setting their own priorities and agenda. A distinctively African feminism should portray women as strong, innovative agents and decision makers in their specific contexts. It should empower African women and work for them in the ways that they want it to.

Women in Nairobi have undergone formidable struggles in the search for space and opportunity in the city. Although the period from the 1960s to the early 1980s was characterized by the ideals of self-governance, these ideals were not particularly geared towards women. Women were not seen as individuals who would bring positive change to the city. Women's issues during this period were left to the social services departments of both the city council and the Ministry of Home Affairs. It was the women's organizations, churches and charities that took a keen interest in addressing issues affecting women. Elite women, by virtue of their education or the fact that their husbands occupied senior positions, felt obliged to incorporate women into the modernity and urbanism project. It was necessary to include women because the exodus from the countryside to the big cities had done a great deal of harm in certain regions. Those who were lucky would find work; others often fell prey to prostitution and delinquency. Here, the economic problem and the social problem were one. It was therefore an urgent matter to create social services that would help stabilize the victims of the mass exodus (Kenya National Archives 1965b).

Elites initiated the struggle for ascendancy by first attempting to understand the source of the problem of women in the city. They observed that women migrants were vulnerable and needed a lot of help. They were inadequately prepared to engage in urban life or to participate in the modernity and urbanism project. This state of affairs was sometimes attributed to the hostility of men in so far as the economic independence of women was concerned, to scarcity of work for women, to the aftermath of colonialism, and sometimes to religion (Kenya National Archives 1965b).

They proposed that the question of women in the city should be interrogated within the broader question of colonialism, modernity and urbanism and the rising social transformation from a basically African society to one based on the ethos of western European values. In the 1960s, there was a general feeling that the women's problem resulted from the fact that they lagged behind in the adoption of modernity. This meant that if women adopted modernity and became active participants in urbanism, their problems would be solved. It was outdated customs and patriarchal control, as well as religion, that held women back. At an African conference in Kindia in Guinea in 1964, Madame Diallo Virginie Kamara observed that:

> The African of yesterday took shelter behind outmoded customs or an absurd fatalism. In certain regions, religions, social traditions, man's dictatorial attitude had left [a] deep impression that she was submissive, resigned, without initiative to speak of the life of the family as well as in the affairs of the city, without sociological status in society, a society which however was in the process of evolution (Kenya National Archives 1965b).

This implied that a woman's adoption of modernity and urbanism was controlled by religion, social traditions and patriarchy, among other things. The combination of these factors denied her voice, not only within the family but also in the city. Women needed to be rescued from this condition in order to become part of the modernity and urbanism project. Madame Kamara further felt that there was a need to promote responsibility and conscience among women and to initiate solidarity between the elite and the unlettered women so that they could work together to break the barriers that were obstructing women's transformation:

> We ought to incorporate all African women with a sense of responsibility and awakening of conscience but above all we ought to break down the barriers which create a dividing wall between the unlettered and the intellectual. It is on these grounds alone that our action will become positive. It will play its part in the awakening of the national conscience and indispensable conditions for reaching [a] concrete result. The African woman should know of the immense possibilities that she has to bring to bear on the destiny of her country (Kenya National Archives 1965b).

The issues of women were also being debated widely in the media. For example, Mrs C. Y. Edwards Olchurie wrote that women in Kenya were on the pathway to change and that this had been occasioned by the fact that the traditionally protective environment that provided women with security in their roles was no longer in existence. This called for women to change with the times.

> The task we are left with now is how to stay within the traditional system and still progress and change with our men and country. Although this is a difficult, challenging task, we women of Kenya must forge ahead and cope with this demanding situation. We must do so because we women give form and substance to the social aspirations of our society (Olchurie 1966).

Without government institutions to address the plight of women, their concerns were left in the hands of charities and trusts or church organizations such as St John's Community Centre, which was run by the Church Missionary Society in the Pumwani area of the city. A British trust took on responsibility for dealing with Pumwani's 12,000 deserted and widowed women and started a centre for printing cloth designs where women could come to work accompanied by their children. The centre grew into a fully fledged factory known as Maridadi Fabrics, with support from the Swedish International Development Agency, Bread for the World (Germany) and World Vision (United States). The factory specialized in African prints and was geared towards serving the tourist market (Pattison 1975).

*Efforts to lift women from the margins* The work of incorporating women into the modernity and urbanism project was left in the hands of the social services division of the city council and women's organizations such as the Kenya Council of Women. The Kenya Council of Women not only saw the need for women to change but was also actively involved in bringing the social transformation of women to modernity and urbanism.

The Kenya Council of Women was an umbrella association that included non-political women's societies in Kenya, including the Young Women's Christian Association, the Girl Guides, Maendeleo ya Wanawake, the East African Women's League, the Asian Women's Association and the Kenyan Muslim Women's Society. The women came together to promote their own welfare and facilitate friendship and understanding between women of different groups as well as to play their part in developing the country and providing voluntary services (Kenya National Archives 1964).

In the 1960s and 1970s, the Kenya Council of Women was particularly concerned about the welfare of women in the country in general and in the city in particular. The council was especially worried about urban women who had no skills and were considered idle. During one meeting held on 12 September 1962, the Professional and Business Women's Society chairperson suggested that, as something had to be done for women whose husbands were employed as domestic servants in the urban areas because they seemed to do nothing the whole day long, there should be help for them to learn sewing or knitting (Kenya National Archives 1964).

One of the ways in which the Kenya Council of Women prompted women's entry into the modernity and urbanism project and laid the groundwork for their becoming part of the capitalist economy was through 'home industries'. The home industries project involved training women to make products from the comfort of their own homes, products that would later be sold in local and international markets. Some of the products promoted included dolls, baskets, garments, mats, rugs, beadwork and hats. The council was also concerned about the changing dynamics among women, such as the issue of single women in employment. It commissioned a survey that illustrated that the number of single women in the city had increased and recommended that the living conditions of single women be improved. It also proposed the need to recognize the important role women were playing in society and the need to compensate women according to the role they played.

The Kenya Council of Women also facilitated training projects in Lang'ata Women's Prison. Most of the women were in prison because of vagrancy or engaging in illegitimate trade, such as the brewing of illicit alcohol and prostitution. The Kenya Council of Women wanted these women equipped with skills that they could use once released from prison. It also proposed that women freed from prison be linked with Maendeleo ya Wanawake's home industries, where they would put their skills into practice.

The Kenya Council of Women, in collaboration with the Kaloleni training centre, also promoted traditional handicraft skills and concepts such as those of the *kiondo* (basket) and fitted them into the modernity project. By so doing, it enlisted the concept of African handicrafts into modern small-scale manufacturing. This was done by initiating new shapes of *kiondo* and introducing new dyes and weaving styles. The council would draw expertise from other countries such as India and Israel, which meant linking this African concept with international ones. Most of the goods produced by these women were geared towards the tourist market and export, which created a subaltern link with international capital. This allowed the women to enter the circuits of capital at the city and global levels. Whether the women gained status or remained at subalternity level by entering into the city and global circuits of capital is another issue altogether. But the purpose of engaging women in home industries was not only to keep them busy, but also to raise their standards of living and improve hygiene in their households.

Women took it upon themselves to bring on board their fellow marginalized colleagues, as is evident in the letter to Vice-President Murumbi shown below:

Dear Mr Murumbi,
We have been very interested to learn of the connection with certain cottage industry projects, and I am writing to advise you of our own eagerness to promote various forms of women's handicrafts, etc., in order to assist them in raising their standard of living.

To this end, the Kenya Council of Women last year formed a committee to investigate the possibilities of encouraging traditional handicrafts and developing them especially for the tourist market. This committee has received considerable encouragement from many quarters, especially from the Maendeleo ya Wanawake of which I am now President.

We do feel, however, that it is important for the progress of our investigation and plans that we cooperate with all other people and people concerned with similar work and we should therefore be most interested to hear from you.

Yours truly,

Mrs Jael Mbogo (Kenya National Archives 1965b)

The women were also actively involved in liaising with different government departments, such as the trade and supplies department of the Ministry of Commerce and Industry, and international development agencies, as well as the Industrial Development Corporation. The eagerness to support women and incorporate them in the modernity and urbanism project corresponded to the ideal of self-governance that characterized the 1960s and 1970s. During these periods, both men and women engaged in the formidable task of trying to get everyone included in the development agenda. A lot of energy and voluntarism was involved among both men and women. Through their organization, women were eager, in the words of Jael Mbogo, to see the status of other women uplifted. The subalterns (*wananchi*), on the other hand, were also responsive and were equally eager to participate in development (Kinyanjui 2012). For everyone, the air exuded the aura of change. This, however, altered in the late 1980s due to the effects of neoliberalism, the effects of the attempted coup in 1982, as well as the emergence of a new type of women's movement.

### The women's struggle: 1990 to 2010

In the 1990s, the national women's organizations such as the National Council of Women (formerly called the Kenya Council of Woman) and Maendeleo ya Wanawake were affected by political interference and were thoroughly weakened. When Maendeleo ya Wanawake was affiliated to the ruling party KANU and became KANU Maendeleo ya Wanawake, it lost its major donors. The National Council of Women was similarly affected by politically initiated leadership problems. The weakening of these organizations greatly affected the representation of subaltern women. Subsequent women's movements that emerged leaned towards rights activism rather than practically addressing unemployment, lack of skills, hygiene and standards of living. The practical agenda of imparting skills and linking women to the circuits of capital within the city that had been propagated in the 1960s and 1970s was slowed down.

The 1990s were a critical period for the women's movement in Kenya. Women's transformation was to come through political and legal reform. Two strong protagonists, Maria Nzomo and Edda Gachukia, were both University of Nairobi lecturers when the women's movement emerged. Maria formed the National Committee on the Status of Women non-governmental organization (NGO), the main agenda of which was the legal and political empowerment of women. She envisioned women taking up power by being parliamentary representatives or even presidents. She even envisaged women having their own political party since the male-dominated parties were shutting out women. She embarked on a journey of holding civic education campaigns for women at the grassroots level and educating them on their rights. Edda Gachukia, on the other hand, advocated for the education of girls through the Forum for African Women Educationists (FAWE). She initiated programmes to support girls in education and to challenge the existing gender-blind school curriculum, the use of masculine images in textbooks and the role of male teachers in girls' education.

The new women's movement coincided with the United Nations Nairobi Forward-looking Strategies in 1985 and the Beijing Platform for Action in 1995. There was a lot of international donor goodwill that supported consultancies, civic education and sensitization of women to gender inequality and rights. This also led to the formation of NGOs that lobbied for women's rights and civic rights. Some gains made included the increased enrolment of girls in school, the passing of the Sexual Violence Act, affirmative action on the representation (up to 30 per cent) of women in organizations, and the incorporation of women's rights in the 2010 constitution. These achievements have enhanced the individual rights of women, and especially of elite women who have the skills and the certificates to compete for bureaucratic jobs with men. However, the rights and interests of subaltern women in the markets and the slums have not been adequately addressed by this movement.

While the women's movement made considerable gains, those gains were not on the same wavelength as those of subaltern women (Anyona 1996). They were deemed elitist. The subaltern women observed that their worldview differed from that of the elite women and that elite women rarely mixed with subaltern women. The main sources of difference between the two groups were income, power and education. While the elite women could sit and challenge the men in the corridors of power, the subaltern women did not have such privileges.

The 'empowerment', 'equality' and 'Beijing Platform for Action' rhetoric that characterized rights awareness and civic education was also viewed as being divorced from transformative action and strategies for women (Mathiu 1998; Ndii 1998; Ngwiri 1998). According to Mathiu (1998), women constitute marginalized souls in Kenya whose welfare is paid lip service to by women and men alike, especially when there is an election to be won or money to make from international donors (Mathiu 1998).

The elite women blamed their failure to reach the subaltern women on a lack of resources and the fact that there were too many subaltern women. The distance between the elite women and the subaltern women perhaps explains the failure of the first woman presidential candidate, Charity Ngilu, to win the election in 1997. The subaltern women, feeling that the elite women were more privileged, failed to support the agenda to have a woman president. This raises the broader question of whether elite women are the right spokespersons for the subaltern women on the streets.

It is worth noting that when women and men hawkers were being harassed in the streets in the 1990s, the women's movement did not pick this as an issue or part of their struggle. The movement was more concerned about getting more women representatives in parliament, on statutory bodies, and in permanent secretary positions. The subaltern women knew very well that they could not get to these positions because of their level of education. They lacked the knowledge and power to acquire these positions.

The lack of solidarity between the subaltern and the elite is perhaps due to the fact that the elite women are advancing a culture of modernity that is beyond the reach of subaltern women. Modernity as envisioned by planners and academics cannot be realized in the spaces in which subaltern women operate. These habitats are isolated from the spaces of power. Modernity cannot occur in the crowded subaltern habitats of Burma or Gikomba Market. These are the spaces of the ordinary culture, characterized by pragmatism and flexibility as well as openness and solidarity. They are driven by the view 'I am because we are and since we are, I am' (Mbiti 1969: 108). They do not have a top-down command strategy that they have to adhere to before taking action. To the subaltern woman, the agenda is shared and expressed in small chats or in song and dance while the agenda of elite women is documented and archived. The agenda of the elite woman is also supported by foreigners, while the subalterns pursue a local agenda.

The struggles in subaltern spaces are basically different from those of the elite women. Subaltern women are concerned with the availability of clean trading spaces, whether they will have enough cash to source stock, whether they will have customers or not. Indeed, one woman reported by Mwakisha (1991) observed that she attended meetings where they raise money for individuals in her own network. This implies that the subaltern women have their own collective organization that they use to advance their own struggles, and the strategy of elite women creating awareness about them may be misconceived and misplaced.

While struggles relating to sexual violence and HIV/AIDS converge for both the elite and the subaltern women, the material aspects of the struggle do not. The elite women enjoy modernity, power and control. They can negotiate with men in statutory boardrooms or in the media. The subaltern women's medium of communication is basically oral or the popular song. It is for this reason that the *kamweretho* dance has become an important medium for subaltern women to articulate their clamour for rights (Kinyanjui and Gichuhi 2010).

The awareness campaigns carried out in workshops and seminars by some feminists working in NGOs and academia do not translate into liberating political action for subaltern women who are concerned with livelihood rights and spatial justice (Abele 1997). In the words of Mwakisha (1991), they are all women but the focus is different. The celebrated women achievers are not those who hew wood or push and pull bags in Wakulima Market to ensure that food from rural areas gets to tables in city hotels and households; those treadling sewing machines in Uhuru Market to ensure that *wananchi* are clothed; or those selling garments in ECT Stalls in Taveta Road. The women achievers are chiefs, lawyers, university professors and educationists (Abele 1997).

In spite of this framing by mainstream development thinking, the subaltern engages in a process of self-transformation. This is because, in the words of Simone (2004: 407), people can act as a type of infrastructure that facilitates the intersection of society, so that expanded spaces of economic and cultural operation become available to residents of limited means. In a way, the people create platforms for reproduction in the city. This is exactly the role that the *mama mboga* (greengrocer) or women garment retailers along Taveta Road perform in the city of Nairobi. In their search for a livelihood, they move and link spaces and people. For example, in the 2011 YU Mobile commercial, the *mama mboga* had crossed borders from her slum or peri-urban location into the space of affluence. Using a mobile phone, she was able to transact business with an Asian woman who was confined to a high-rise building in a gated community. A large majority of subaltern women involved in garment making, retail trade in food or clothing, food preparation or domestic services cross the borders created by the planning and political elite and connect with people in other spaces.

The movement of women in economic informality from the margin to the centre has to be led by the women themselves. They have to make certain conscious decisions about the manner in which to engage in livelihood negotiation in economic informality, adopt strategies and define the path that they will follow to reach the centre.

# 5 | Women, mobility and economic informality

The movement of women in economic informality from rural areas, slums, informal settlements and peri-urban locations is critical to overcoming their material deprivation. This movement involves physical, social and abstract translocation. In their habitat in rural areas, the slum, informal settlement or peri-urban location, women in economic informality are boxed in by patriarchal norms and values that limit their access to the circuits of labour, capital and power. Moving to production spaces in the city of Nairobi allows the women to engage in entrepreneurial activities as well as obtain new ideas and information.

By moving into the delineated production spaces in the city, the women, through mingling with other city dwellers and workers and observation, acquire new ideas and information that can lead to changes in the way they do things. Thus, a walk or a matatu ride into the city may mean a transformative and liberative experience or the opening up of space and opportunity to fulfil livelihood goals. Mobility becomes a source of women's agency to be proactive in livelihood matters.

## Women and mobility

The mobility of women in communities and cities is regulated; societies in most parts of the world have a history of controlling and regulating female physical mobility. While control of movement may be associated with women's insecurity outside the home environment, there are also fears that women who move out of the home are likely to engage in 'immoral activities' or that they might do so at the expense of family duties. In some communities, women are not supposed to move out of their homes without an accompanying brother or other male relative.

In the colonial period, women's movement in the city was controlled on the grounds of morality and colonial labour policies that preferred men over women. Only a few women in the early days dared to move to the city and engage in trade; the women who did dare to move into the city had the tenacity to overcome the barriers that controlled movement and struggled to be incorporated into the city's modernizing process in order to claim citizenship (Schlyter 2009).

Mobility is often neglected as a factor in improving women's conditions in cities in Kenya. While most efforts have been directed towards reproductive health, the creation of enterprises, domestic and sexual violence and access to education, the way in which women make physical movements between spaces in the city is often disregarded, yet mobility enhances participation in economic activities. For women to reap the benefits of the city, they must move within and across the city spaces in pursuit of the flows of power, capital, ideas and information. In particular, women must move into spaces of action in the city.

Cities in both the global North and the global South always tend to segregate people on the basis of class or race and discourage movement between these spaces. They also have private and public spaces. People and goods have to cross borders to get into these spaces, and this flow of people and goods between spaces has been the essence of the urban experience and the survival of the city. Graham and Marvin (2001), quoted in Sheller (2004), describe cities as spaces of 'networked urbanism' where people, vehicles and information flow through human, technological and informational mobility infrastructures.

Mobility as a source of dynamism for people in the informal setting in general, and women in economic informality in particular, has been largely neglected. This has meant that the movement of a large proportion of people who move to transfer objects, information and ideas in the city has been disregarded. Mobility is critical to social change because people, objects, information and ideas are mobilized through it (Büscher and Urry 2009). The mobility of women is equally important for building women's agency and subsequent empowerment. Jirón (2010) emphasizes the importance of women's mobility:

> Leaving the house starts being a way of changing life, and independence. Going out is important for many women, having a routine outside their house, making money, even if it means going out to do the same thing at someone else's house: clean and take care of children. Having money means more independence and it makes working very important. The journey is a crossing for them, a gateway to something new (Jirón 2010: 76).

In particular, mobility provides women with independence and openings for new opportunities.

Mobility releases people from their spatial confinement and is a strategy for social inclusion because it overcomes constraints of space at particular moments to access networks of leisure, work, friendship and family (Cass et al. 2005). In Nairobi, city zoning policies isolate and confine individuals to specific spaces in the city. Slums, informal settlements and peri-urban locations are the least accessible spaces in the city. Often, there are no roads or streets that directly link these spaces to the city's production spaces, and, even if they are there, the links are impassable and usually congested with traffic.

The lack of accessibility and free movement entrenches the subordination and marginalization of people in these spaces. Whereas the Aga Khan–Highridge area in Nairobi is well connected with roads to the upmarket suburbs

64

of Westlands, Runda and Kitisuru, there are no direct roads that link, for example, Mathare slum with the Aga Khan–Highridge area. Many of the traders, domestic workers and security guards working in Highridge and Aga Khan and living in Mathare and Mlango Kubwa use a footpath that enters Karura Forest below the former Pangani petrol station. The path traverses City Park and goes into the hawkers' market and the Aga Khan–Highridge area. If these people were to travel by vehicle, they would first take a matatu into the city centre and then take another one that plies Limuru Road. Forest Road and Muthaiga Road, which link the Aga Khan–Highridge area with Mathare and Mlango Kubwa, are closed to matatu transport because they traverse spaces where the 'who's who' of diplomatic circles live, as well as the elite. Yet these are the spaces where the subalterns go to look for work.

In some African contexts, for example among the Agĩkũyũ community, women belong to the portable or mobile gender (*mũndũ wa nja*) and are not confined to a specific space. The space of their birth is not necessarily the space where they will eventually live and die. They move and get married or, in the case of difficulties in marriage, can divorce and return to their parents or marry someone else. Thus, mobility is fundamental to the female gender and should not be taken for granted. While women could move from their family in the case of marriage, among the Agĩkũyũ, women's movement is condoned only if it is functional. In the traditional Agĩkũyũ society, women moved out of the home to perform tasks such as collecting firewood, water or food for the family. This was done mostly in the company of other women. However, women who made many physical movements were frowned upon and considered immoral or 'manly'. They would be labelled if they were renowned for travelling regularly and would be given names outside their clan names, such as *Nyang'endo* (one who travels a lot), *Nyagũthiĩ* (habitual traveller) or *Njeri* (one who adventures or likes making visits).

The importance of mobility to the individual was also greatly acknowledged in proverbs; however, these referred to the mobility of the male gender. For example, *Kagũrũ keime gatihana ke mũhu* (wet feet are different from ones covered by ashes) signifies that a person who spends time out of the house is likely to be different in socioeconomic status from one who sits by the fireside warming his feet; it encourages people to go out to the farm or to graze rather than sit at home doing nothing.

The critical role that mobility plays for gender was realized as early as 1895 in America when Frances Willard learned to ride a bicycle at the age of 53 (Hanson 2010).

> By learning to ride a bicycle, Willard regained her lost mobility after many years of being trapped in decorous middle class womanhood. The freedom of movement it provided her is bound up with an exhilarating feeling of confidence and accomplishment and a sense of expanded possibilities,

aspirations and personal growth, not to mention an upright moral character (Hanson 2010: 6).

A study carried out in Benin and Guatemala reinforces the importance of mobility for gender. Mandel (2004) observes that mobility has significant influence in Porto Novo, Benin, on the scale of women's entrepreneurial activities and the type of goods they trade in. In particular, mobility helps the women overcome the lack of basic facilities. In the Guatemala study, Sundberg (2004) documents the mobility of one woman that led to the formation of Agrupacion. Agrupacion enabled the women to have business priorities that were beyond their immediate families. It provided them with 'somewhere to go' where they could engage in something different.

For many generations, urban transport has been closely linked to the development of the capitalist economy in the city. Transportation links individuals with the labour market and the home. According to Law (1999: 571), 'the work trip is the single human activity that most clearly bridges the symbolic and spatial distinction between public and private which is a feature of western urbanism'. In this sense, urbanism in Nairobi is not very different from urbanism in the West. Residential areas that constitute the private domain are separated from productive spaces in the centre of the city and in the industrial area. In one way or another, main road arteries and streets are all directed towards the central business district (CBD) and the industrial area.

While, when viewed through a patriarchal lens, moving between the residential and the productive spaces is supposedly natural for the male labour force, it does not come easy for women in general and subaltern women in particular. Women are also said to use transport differently from their male counterparts in terms of trip distance, choice of transport mode and trip purpose, among other differences (Law 1999). Women use transport differently because of household responsibilities, their position in the labour market, socialization, income, vulnerability and their relationship with men (see Bueuret 1991; Lang 1992; Little 1994; quoted in Law 1999). Women's mobility is constrained by patriarchy, gender roles and the masculine-oriented planning and political elites. Women make shorter trips because of their nurturing responsibilities (Hanson 2010).

## Mobility of women in economic informality

This chapter interrogates the means of movement of women in economic informality into the productive spaces within the different social spatial forms. Despite existing regulations on women's mobility in Nairobi, women have not been held down. They move across different socio-spatial urban forms, as illustrated by the 2011 YU Mobile television commercial showing a woman in economic informality hawking vegetables in a high-income residential area of Nairobi.

Women move to become domestic workers, babysitters, vegetable vendors or kiosk owners in the upper-income neighbourhoods, street traders in Muthurwa or in garment exhibitions along Taveta Road, or garment makers and retailers in Kenyatta, Jericho, Uhuru and Gikomba Markets. Some of the women make international travel to other African cities and global South cities such as Istanbul and Shanghai to source trade goods such as shoes, bags, garments and electronics. Essentially, the movement to these spaces serves as the basis for their transformation and liberation. Echoing the importance of mobility as transformative and liberative, one of the respondents to the survey had this to say about her passport, which enables her to travel abroad to purchase clothing for her stall in Nairobi:

> My passport has transformed me from a mere primary school teacher to a woman who owns property. I am in control of my life, my household economy and the future of my children. I have educated all my children up to the university level under the self-sponsored parallel programme.

According to the survey on women in informal economy, over a quarter (31.9 per cent or 104) of the women operating businesses in the city markets live in slums (Table 5.1). Almost a quarter of the women (71 or 21.7 per cent) have their residences in the peri-urban locations of Kangemi, Dagoretti, Uthiru and Ruiru. Less than a quarter of them (59 or 18.3 per cent) live in the emerging settlements of Kayole, Zimmerman, Githurai and Ruai. Others live in the low-income neighbourhoods of Umoja and Eastleigh (57 or 17.4 per cent) while a few (35 or 10.7 per cent) live in the middle-income neighbourhoods of Golf Course, Nairobi West, Buruburu and Langata.

To facilitate movement, women in the informal economy need capital to start their businesses. The survey data revealed that the start-up capital was as low as KSh 500 but could reach KSh 80,000. Women obtained their start-up capital

TABLE 5.1 The location of informal economy women's residences in Nairobi

| Area of residence | Number | Percentage |
| --- | --- | --- |
| Slum | 104 | 31.9 |
| Peri-urban | 71 | 21.7 |
| Informal | 59 | 18.3 |
| Low income | 57 | 17.4 |
| Middle income | 35 | 10.7 |
| *Total* | 326 | 100 |

*Source*: Author's survey, 2012.

TABLE 5.2 Sources of start-up capital of Nairobi women in the informal economy

| Source | Number | Percentage |
|---|---|---|
| Spouse | 86 | 26.8 |
| Relative | 85 | 26.5 |
| Business | 59 | 18.4 |
| *Chama* | 54 | 16.8 |
| Microfinance | 30 | 9.3 |
| Church self-help group | 7 | 2.2 |
| *Total* | 321 | 100 |

*Source*: Author's survey, 2012.

from a variety of sources, as indicated in Table 5.2. Almost equal proportions of women sourced their start-up capital from their spouse (26.8 per cent or 86 of the women) or a relative (26.5 per cent or 85). This means that members of the extended family are an important source of support, while some spouses support women in their endeavours. The next most important source for start-up capital was the woman's alternative business (18.4 per cent or 59). This was followed by the *chama* or social group (16.8 per cent or 54). Microfinance sources that provided start-up capital accounted for only 9.3 per cent (30), while church self-help groups were also important sources of finance for starting informal businesses for a small number of women (2.2 per cent or 7).

The women move from their localities to work sites located in different parts of the city. They move in order to derive livelihoods; movement within the city is a phenomenon of agency. According to one woman:

> I used to sit in the house all day until my husband gave me some money to start selling clothes. The difference between staying at home and going to work is like that between day and night. It has enabled me to move out of the home and do something. Going out has exposed me to a lot of opportunities and challenges. My perception of life has changed. I have discovered that there is more I can do to change my living standards.

This means that movement changes the socioeconomic perspective of a woman. It is a step forward in a woman's social transformation and liberation and sets the stage for a woman to engage in productive action. On further probing, the woman identified financial independence, being occupied and the creation of a social space as the benefits of working. Financial independence and empowerment are critical to a woman's well-being. They free her from reliance on hand-outs and set her on the path towards managing her own poverty and that of her household. For generations the powerlessness of women has hinged on their lack of access to and control of money. Thus, being able to access and control money is a step towards transformation and liberation. A financially empowered woman is able to purchase goods and meet her own needs as well as the needs of the family. Financial empowerment also improves her bargaining power in the household economy as she contributes to the family kitty. Hitherto, a woman would present her budget to her spouse who would then choose the amount to give her. As a recipient, the woman had no say on the management of the family finances. As one woman put it: 'I am now able to sit at the table with my spouse and discuss family expenditure.' Another woman stated that she was able to generate her own income and manage her needs. She had stopped relying on hand-outs from well-wishers and her spouse.

While the work of stay-at-home mothers should not be underestimated, some women felt that the ability to leave home and work in the public space made them more meaningfully occupied. In the African rural context, women have been known to work for long hours on family farms while the benefits of farming go to the male spouse. In the urban context, where there is little farming, a stay-at-home mother has no farm or source of income. Further, in slums and peri-urban locations, most of the women live in either single-roomed houses or two-roomed houses where housework is limited. After sending their children to school in the morning, if there is no washing to do a woman may have nothing to do in the house. The situation is made worse by the fact that there are no libraries, museums, parks or shops in the neighbourhood where one can spend time in between household chores. Women living in these conditions consider themselves idle in between household chores, as exemplified by the woman's testimony below:

> I used to spend long boring days. After doing the morning chores, I found myself with nothing else to do. I would chat with neighbours, chatting that always ended up in gossip. This always bred conflict, especially when the subject of the gossip got wind of it. I decided that this trend had to stop and opted to do something more fulfilling and liberating. After much thought, I settled on starting a business venture that would allow me to be in contact with people and make meaningful exchanges. Since I did not have start-up capital, I requested my sister to give me some money. She was kind enough to do this and my life in business was born. I moved into Gikomba Market and my life has never been the same.

Work outside the home is greatly valued by development practitioners. Indeed, most gender-and-development activities call for increased women's education so that they can move into the world of work. Women are also encouraged to have fewer children so that they can participate in the labour force. In the urban setting, educated women and those with fewer children find staying at home a tormenting lifestyle. Working is not only associated with earning an income, it provides psychological and sociological benefits too. It also symbolizes that the woman is 'modern'. And, after all, for most people the goal in migrating to Nairobi city is to look for work, and unemployment in the city is considered a problem that should be solved. Therefore, women, like their male counterparts, long for something to do outside the home. Being able to move out of these residential spaces to a business in the city centre provides a woman with a worthwhile occupation that enhances her self-image. It helps women feel that they are gainfully employed, which is good for their self-actualization. One woman observed that she had something to do for profit rather than idling, while another stated that her mind was kept busy. These women felt that they were doing something worthwhile rather than the routine work of homemaking, which is rarely appreciated or rewarded. They were active in the city and were engaging in something they were proud of.

The CBD in Nairobi is the most lucrative part of the city. It is where most purchasing power is concentrated and is the space in which most people aspire to situate their businesses. Most people in slums, informal settlements and peri-urban locations move out to search for work early in the morning: if one had a business in the informal or peri-urban settlements, only a handful of people would come to buy during the day, although businesses pick up in the evening when people return from work. Further, people visiting Nairobi for shopping from other parts of the country are also unlikely to go to slums, peri-urban locations or informal settlements to shop because of their inaccessibility and lack of security.

The street in the CBD is different. Apart from the human traffic, it is clean and has space for meeting new or old acquaintances. It is a space for observing and meeting other cultures. It is the space where women learn about fashion and obtain new ideas as well as information. It is a space for forming new relationships.

Thus, going out into the CBD creates opportunities for new social spaces of engagement with different people. As one woman put it: 'Being away from home is educative. Hardly do I stay in the shop without meeting someone new who will tell me something I did not know about before.' Another woman said that, in the CBD: 'I interact with different people – both young and old – from different tribes. It is different from my peri-urban location where I only meet neighbours.' The flow of ideas between the CBD and the peri-urban setting explains the dynamism in the latter. In this case, the women are serving as the conduits for the flow of information and capital between the two spaces. Their day-to-day experiences in the CBD are reproduced in the slums, informal settlements and peri-urban locations.

In the new spaces in the CBD, the women also form *vyama* (social groups) with other women informal workers, and this enlarges their latitude for socioeconomic engagement. This in turn enhances their transformation and liberation.

These new spaces will, perhaps in the future, form the nuclei for women's participation in public life and the feminization of the centre of town.

## Modes of movement

Women use public means of transport more frequently than personal cars (Crane and Takahashi 2009). Table 5.3 corroborates these studies by showing that only 8.2 per cent or 26 of the women in economic informality in the survey used their personal car to travel to their business spaces in the city. Some of the women bought a car after engaging in the informal economy while others used their husband's car. Although the act of women walking to work is seen as a constraint and a testimony of their marginalization, a quarter (81 or 25.6 per cent) of the women in economic informality walked from their homes to the delineated business spaces. Despite the fact that walking is energy- and time-consuming, it is a form of empowering strategy for the women: it is definitely better than being confined in the slums, informal settlement or peri-urban locations where opportunities for deriving livelihoods are limited. By making the effort to walk, the women show that they do not want to be constrained by immobility accruing from gender ideologies or limited resources. It is better to make any move than to make none at all.

Women in economic informality using public transport in Nairobi have the choice of using the matatu (a 14-seater Nissan van). Slightly over half (179 or 56.5 per cent) of them used the matatu to move from their homes to delineated production spaces in the CBD. Only 28 or 8.8 per cent used the minibus, which is cheaper but slower than the matatu. However, studies have documented the high degree of violence and sexual abuse that occurs in matatu transport: indeed, matatu entrepreneurs are viewed by commuters as thugs who exploit and mistreat their passengers (Mutongi 2006).

TABLE 5.3 Means of transport used by women to move between their residence and the city

| Means of transport | Number of women | Percentage |
|---|---|---|
| Matatu | 179 | 56.5 |
| Walking | 81 | 25.6 |
| Minibus | 28 | 8.8 |
| Personal car | 26 | 8.2 |
| Pick-up | 2 | 0.6 |
| Motorcycle | 1 | 0.3 |
| *Total* | 317 | 100 |

*Source*: Author's survey, 2012.

Why would women overwhelmingly choose such a violent mode of transport? The obvious answer would relate to its affordability, convenience and the fact that the matatus are fast. But hidden in this answer is the fact that the matatu crews are also part of the general subaltern struggle in Kenya. Women resonate with this struggle. The matatu site is a site of *gũkua na mariũka* (death or collapse as well as revival and resurrection). It is a site of both hope and despair. This is the essence of any struggle, be it political or economic.

The women consider the matatu ride an experience of reinvention and self-discovery as well as one of hope and taking risks. These are experiences that women in economic informality identify with in their daily livelihood struggles. The livelihood struggle comprises ups and downs; it involves negotiating corners, going uphill sometimes while at other times it is a smooth ride, especially when all the factors of production are available. The matatu ride epitomizes the struggle that men and women in economic informality experience every day in their livelihood negotiation.

The matatu is also a forum where the subaltern struggle is discussed, with issues ranging from politics and food shortages to corruption. Narratives of failure and success are related in the matatu. In addition, messages or slogans posted on the matatu inform and energize: for example, on one matatu that plies the Dandora route, a message posted on its bodywork reads '*demokrasia ni ukoloni wa kisasa*' (democracy is a form of neo-colonialism), while a matatu on the Kahawa route bears the message 'History repeats itself, opportunity comes once'. These messages are a reminder of the everyday struggles in which subalterns are involved, and they provide women with the agency to resist subordination by patriarchy and the masculine planning elite.

The matatu is indeed a solidarity base for subalterns. The music played in them, the videos screened and the radio talks broadcast provide women travellers with new information and engagement strategies on a range of issues, including sexual rights and resistance. This makes a matatu ride a springboard towards liberation, transformation and subaltern survival strategies. Thus, rather than being a nuisance, the matatu becomes a space of positive energy for subaltern women's everyday struggles.

The benefits that the women in the case study have realized by moving range from personal autonomy, financial independence and the learning of new ideas and lifestyles to the ability to chart their future and that of their families. The inability of a woman to control her future is, perhaps, the worst form of denial of her human rights. Women who have no income and rely solely on the male spouse could be subjects of relocation and displacement from the city at any time. Their stay in the city is dependent on their husbands' decisions. However, women are claiming their future and that of their children through daily trips to the CBD. With an income and an activity in the city, they can decide to stay on even in the event that their husband retires or expires, while single parents are able to provide for themselves and their children.

Mobility has rescued these women from isolation in peri-urban locations where there is limited infrastructure and choice. Although the women are occupying stalls or kiosks in the city, mobility has situated them in the centre of information, news and capital and the gains are immense. In turn, this will serve as the beginning of an indigenous women's movement rather than one where some women apportion themselves the responsibility of 'rescuing' subaltern women from subaltern men while they strive to maintain their privileged positions. Thus, enhancing women's mobility across and within the city could be the key to achieving the desired goals of women's empowerment and equity.

# 6 | Women in economic informality in Nairobi

As shown in Chapter 2, urbanization in Nairobi owes its origin to the construction of the Kenya–Uganda railway and the subsequent establishment of a railway station, an administration centre and a bazaar. It was not driven by factory workshop manufacturing or by Fordist mass production like urbanization in Europe and North America. Also, the new cultural economy of post-Fordist Europe and North America does not seem to be taking place in Nairobi. This is mainly due to the fact that colonial cities were supposed to be bulking spaces for raw materials for export and markets for manufactured goods from the mother country. Further, industrial policy has not been a priority in the postcolonial city. Postcolonial cities have not been able to wean themselves off their traditional roles as defined during colonialism. Industrial policy planning in Kenya is largely a central government concern rather than something that is addressed by the city of Nairobi.

Women came to the city either to live with their husbands or to seek employment. Women migrants were dislocated from their roles of production in the household economy in rural areas, as noted in Chapter 4. In the rural areas, women used to contribute to the family economy through subsistence farming and crafts such as basket weaving, pottery, bead making and beer brewing. They also participated in trade where items such as earthenware pots, grains, beads and ornaments or tobacco were exchanged. Women who moved to the city found themselves relegated to the roles of reproduction, housekeeping and minding children as their male counterparts went to work in factories or shops to earn the family's living wage. On the other hand, this reproductive role renewed the urban labour force. Since they could not find jobs in the cities, they tried adopting some of the roles they had performed in rural areas, such as brewing and selling cooked foods, vegetables, fruit and fish. They also traded in grains, handicrafts and garments. The women drew a livelihood strategy from their cultural background. These women's trading activities still survive in the city today and constitute part of the endeavours of economic informality.

This means that economic informality for women constitutes a socio-cultural logic of managing poverty and creating employment. It is also a strategy for inclusion in the urbanism project. However, as shown in Chapter 3, city authorities have been reluctant to promote and advance economic informality as a strategy for urbanization. As a result, it has been left to its own devices to evolve and sprawl in the city. The assumption was that economic informality would be replaced by modernization or by the thriving of large capital.

## The literature on women in economic informality

The participation of women in economic informality has attracted a lot of debate among scholars. The first point of debate relates to its juxtaposition with the formal sector. According to Hart (1973), the informal sector comprises a 'passive exploited majority' who are not able to realize any formidable growth or accumulate wealth. As a result, there is a need for development policies to formalize the informal sector so that it can realize growth, benefit its participants and exit the peripheral economic base. Moser (1978), using a Marxian perspective, illustrates the weakness of the informal sector. She argues that the sector is articulated as part of the capitalist mode of production, which means that women participating in economic informality are disguised proletariats with no autonomy. Moreover, since economic informality is not counted in government statistics, women's role in and contribution to the national economy or to the urban one largely remain invisible. This is because women's activities are often excluded from national census of production surveys and are not accounted for in the calculation of gross national product.

It is also argued that women in economic informality are exploited and work for their husbands as invisible labour that is underpaid. According to Jennings (1994), men control women's productive resources by commanding their unpaid labour as wives and homemakers. This implies that women have no control of their participation in the informal economy. They also lack modern inputs for performing in the informal economy; in particular, they lack credit and the skills required to run businesses. Fapohunda (2012) observes that women have limited access to critical resources such as education, land, technology and credit, which are necessary ingredients for business growth. According to some observations, poor women employed in the informal sector face serious health problems and safety risks, including dangerous working conditions, gendered violence and increased susceptibility to HIV/AIDS (Chant and Pedwell 2008). Nte (2010) observed that women in the urban informal economy in Nigeria experienced a high level of insecurity; this included evictions, expulsions, confiscation of merchandise by local authorities as well as sexual harassment. This was also true in Nairobi, especially with regard to hawkers (Kamunyori 2007).

Further, most women tend to be positioned at the bottom of the informal-sector pyramid or in the intermediate layers. At the bottom of the pyramid, they serve as industrial outworkers or homeworkers, while in the intermediate sectors, they are casual wage workers or operate on their own account (Chen 2007). Women tend to fare poorly in terms of earnings from the informal sector. Chen

(2007) observes that there are differences in men's and women's earnings in the informal sector because men have better working sites and tools and have greater access to productive assets and financial capital, while in some instances men produce higher volumes than women.

Other commentators on economic informality observe that members are not always organized. Since they are mostly not organized or unionized, the women have no voice in matters affecting them or their participation in economic informality. In addition, in cases where the women traders are organized, the leaders of street trader organizations are mainly men (Skinner 2008).

There are, however, other commentators, including Simone (2004), who note that despite the marginality and the non-modern nature of economic informality, basic needs such as food and housing in a large number of African cities, Nairobi included, are provided for by the informal economy. Simone argues that it is pointless to characterize the informal economy as dysfunctional because economic informality is the strategy on which many Africans rely.

For a large majority of people, participation in economic informality is what they know and do best, and it may also be what their parents did. Individuals have to strive to create jobs for themselves outside the official domains of job creation in areas such as large-scale manufacturing or bureaucracy. These individuals, by starting small businesses, strive to come out of a poverty to which they have largely been destined by the urbanization process. By doing so, individuals become actors not only in their own job creation but in the making of the city. This process has generated the phenomenon in African cities that is widely known as economic informality, and women have not been left out of this process. These single initiatives have generated a rubric of an urban form that is an enigma in cities in Africa. Hart (1973) coined the term 'informal economy' to describe this phenomenon that he observed in Accra. The International Labour Organization (ILO) adopted the terminology and carried out a full-scale study of micro and small businesses in Nairobi in 1972. Since then, the ILO has been preoccupied with the concept and formalization of the informal economy in order to make it part and parcel of African cities' employment programmes. The success of this project has been elusive, however. The informal economy continues to sprawl in African cities and has been transforming gradually.

What then drives or spurs the informal economy in African cities? An understanding of the raison d'être of the informal economy must be seen in the context of the desire for self-governance in politics and the economy that imbued many nationalist struggles against colonialism and the concomitant capitalist enterprise. Mbiti (1969), while documenting the change brought about by colonialism on individuals, observes that colonialism plunged individuals into situations where corporate existence had no meaning. Individuals were dehumanized and relegated to working in the mines, in industries and in cities. As a result, they lost the power to own and manage their lives or to negotiate livelihoods, a power that was typical of the African traditional society. In a large majority of precolonial African societies, individuals worked for themselves; waged employment was largely unknown. Colonialism upset this relationship and people were drawn into plantations, mines, industry and cities to work for someone else. This kind of work was dehumanizing. The goal for self-governance was to regain the earlier position of individuals working for themselves, which also involved making livelihood negotiation part of their way of life.

Self-governance for people in economic informality involves managing one's life and engaging in meaningful production. It is the opposite of being dehumanized in waged labour in the settler farm, industry, mine or city. For urban women, self-governance meant reunification with their husbands in the city as well as the restoration or reassertion of their role as managers, custodians and producers in the household economy. This role had been taken away from them by colonialism, which had allocated men the primary role of being the breadwinners in the family and made women recipients of male benevolence.

For men, entry into the informal economy is normal because patriarchy assigns them the role of breadwinners. The entrepreneurial trait is viewed as an entitlement for men because they are motivated by big ideas to become their own bosses and to be independent or they have a knack for identifying opportunities. According to Robertson (1997), the problems women were experiencing in the rural areas forced them to move into the bean trade in the city. Society's perception of women as consumers and recipients of goods bestowed upon them by their husbands and the state has hidden their innate entrepreneurial acumen. Women have resisted this stereotyping and have started their own businesses, albeit informal ones.

In sub-Saharan Africa, in the early 2000s over 84 per cent of women and 63 per cent of men were employed in the informal sector as a percentage of women's and men's non-agricultural employment (ILO 2002). In Kenya, the proportion of women in informal employment as a percentage of non-agricultural employment was 83 per cent and that of men was 59 per cent (ILO 2002). This clearly indicates that a good number of women engage in economic informality. Two questions concerning women in economic informality arise: what are their characteristics? And is their participation liberating or empowering?

Whatever the historical or gender factors that influenced their entry into economic informality, some women explain it with religious anecdotes, as illustrated in the quote below:

> God blessed the 2,000 shillings I was given to start a business. I would travel
> to markets in different parts of the country – Kericho, Kitale, Bungoma,
> and Kisumu. God protected me and made sure I returned safely knowing
> the danger on Kenya's roads. He also blessed me with what I deserved. Over
> time I started my own shop in Kariobangi, bought a stall and then moved

to Gikomba where I did good business till I moved to Ngara and then here, where I am, along Dubois Road.

Another respondent to the survey asserted: 'This business is a success because God blessed my efforts.' Still recognizing divine intervention, a further trader says: 'I was desperate but God showed me the way through a friend. She invited me to share the table she used to lay out her wares. He blessed the little money I was making.'

Yet another informal trader stated:

In everything, I placed God first and tithed according to the rules of my church. Without God, this business would not be where it is. I clean and tidy my shop every morning and then start with a prayer. This is something I have communicated to my employees. Every day they must put God first. I will not tell you how much I tithe. I tithe by supplying fresh flowers to our church every Sunday. It costs me quite a lot of money.

## Women's characteristics and role in economic informality

The women are drawn to economic informality by gender factors and by historical or perceived opportunities in economic informality. Women in economic informality are not a homogeneous category: they are drawn from many backgrounds and vary in terms of age and education.

According to the survey of women in economic informality in Nairobi, the women's ages ranged from 20 to 65 years, with a mean age of 33 years. The mean age is fairly low compared with that found by Ngau and Keino (1996), where the women's mean age in different economic informality spaces was as follows: Kariokor 40.2; Burma 38.4; and Wakulima 37.1. With regard to education, 45.1 per cent or 146 of the women were educated up to secondary school level of education while 26.5 per cent or 86 of the women had a college certificate or diploma. Some 23.8 per cent or 77 of the women had received primary school education, while 1.5 per cent had a university education. Women without any education comprised 3.1 per cent (10). These figures indicate that economic informality is no longer the preserve of women without education or with low levels of education.

Women in economic informality in this survey have relatively high levels of education compared with those in surveys carried out in the 1990s. For example, Ngau and Keino (1996) reported that the majority of women running informal businesses had primary school education (44 per cent), followed by secondary school education (35 per cent) and illiterate (21 per cent). The statistics on education are an indicator that the informal economy is becoming a competitive arena in terms of education. It is not just the illiterate who are venturing into economic informality; the relatively well educated are also moving in.

Fifty-three case studies, drawn mainly from Taveta Road, were carried out to supplement the information provided by the survey of respondents. Data from these case studies revealed that half of the women (50.9 per cent or 27) were married while 49.1 per cent were single. The proportion of single women is comparatively higher than in Ngau and Keino's (1996) study. These characteristics of women in economic informality indicate that women are also changing. Young, educated and single women are all gaining entry into the informal economy. This in turn is likely to have a bearing on the nature of firms, the sourcing of funding, and the general running of businesses.

In terms of the degree of formality, women engaged in economic informality in the survey had made considerable efforts to register their businesses as sole proprietorships or partnerships. The main legal status of the businesses was sole proprietorship (59.1 per cent or 191), while partnerships made up only 6.2 per cent (20 women). Women who had not registered their businesses with the council or with the registrar of societies comprised 34.7 per cent or 112. This level of registration indicates the willingness of women to comply with the rule of law by having their businesses recognized either by the city council or by the registrar of societies. The businesses had a mean age of 14 years, with a range between one and 46 years; this indicates that these businesses could be a lifetime occupation for the women.

In terms of location, the women had positioned their businesses outside the private sphere of their homes. The majority of the businesses were situated in city council designated markets (57.6 per cent or 186) while 26.6 per cent (86) were located by the roadside. Some 6.5 per cent of the women (21) had situated their businesses in the central business district (CBD) while 5.6 per cent had established them in designated *jua kali* sites. Only a negligible proportion of women had located their businesses on river banks or in residential houses. The most interesting finding in this data on location is the situation of women's informal businesses in the CBD. Historically, the CBD has been a site for male entrepreneurs, mainly of Asian origin who employed African men. This is an indicator that women are going beyond the sex-based division of labour that confines them to be homeworkers in slums, informal settlements and peri-urban locations.

The size of working capital for women's businesses in economic informality ranged from KSh 500 to KSh 500,000. Most of the women in the case study relied on their own businesses as a source of working capital (76.2 per cent or 240) while 7.9 per cent (25) relied on the *chama*. Only 7.0 per cent (22) relied on a relative, while 3.5 per cent (11) sourced working capital from their spouse. The proportion of women depending on microfinance as a source of working capital was 5.1 per cent (16), while those relying on church self-help groups constituted 0.3 per cent (just one). This finding is important in the sense that women with businesses in economic informality are self-financing, but, if they want to use external finance, they use the *chama*, a social grouping of women. There is less dependence on spouses or relatives, or even on microfinance strategies that are meant to improve the economic situation of women. This is perhaps due to the entry of women with higher levels of education. The self-financing of women in business is indicative of their movement towards self-autonomy and empowerment. In addition, the businesses are requiring higher amounts of capital than would otherwise be expected for survival businesses.

Another important indicator of women in economic informality's move towards empowerment is their ability to participate in the Nairobi stock exchange. Some women had made investments in shares on the stock exchange – the worth of these shares ranged from KSh 500 to KSh 300,000 – while others had managed to buy plots in the city whose worth ranged from KSh 10,000 to KSh 1 million. In addition, another category of women had constructed rental houses worth KSh 200,000 to KSh 1 million, while others had invested in land in rural areas worth KSh 30,000 to KSh 2 million. Most of the women were unwilling to reveal information about their assets and it is likely that there are more women who own property or land than the survey suggests.

Moreover, a third of the women (33.8 per cent or 106) own their business premises while 24.2 per cent (76) own their own residences. According to a key informant, women in economic informality are able to own property by making savings in a *chama* where they encourage each other to save and buy property or invest. They also alert each other when cheap plots are available for purchase. For example, in one group, the members forfeited lunch for a number of days and used the lunch money saved to buy plots in Githurai in the 1990s. They also alert each other when registration of land-buying companies is taking place. Some informal land-selling companies also make arrangements with the informal market traders so that they can pay for plots in instalments, while other market traders' associations, such as the Marafiki Sacco in Wakulima, have loan facilities for the traders. The *vyama* provide synergy for making investments and continuing with informality as a way of life (Kinyanjui 2012).

Some women in economic informality are also employers of labour. No less than 46 per cent or 153 of the enterprises surveyed were employing workers. The number of workers ranged from one to twelve. This indicates that the businesses are moving from owner-run entities to businesses that call for a division of labour between the owner and the employees. The value of women's businesses in economic informality ranges between KSh 2,500 and KSh 5 million. The high business capital values and the fact that women are employing workers are indicators that businesses are transforming from own-account traders to solid businesses that lie hidden under the rubric of informality.

## Implications for participation in economic informality

It is also important to note that women are playing a critical role in the household economy by paying school fees, buying food, paying rent, and supporting parents or even husbands. Women in economic informality spend between KSh 500 and KSh 100,000 per year in fees for their children's education. They also spend between KSh 100 and KSh 25,000 a month on food; between KSh 500 and KSh 35,000 on rent in a month; and between KSh 500 and KSh 30,000 in supporting parents in a year. The women also spend between KSh 1,000 and KSh 3,000 in supporting their husbands per month. The women's ability to spend money on the household is an important life experience. It shows that they are active participants in the urban household economy and that they do not depend solely on the benevolence of their spouses or relatives. This is both empowering and liberating for the women. It gives them confidence and entitlement in the household. The women derive pride from being able to do something for themselves and for the household and from not having to rely on donations. According to one woman, 'this market space is my farm where I grow provisions for my family. It has made me independent.'

Although most of the women began their entrepreneurial endeavours from marginal positions and spaces, they have moved to the centre and have become shrewd business people whose success is measured by their ability to mediate and manage life in the city as well as to claim citizenship in it. They not only nurture but have also become entrepreneurial, able to build and own a home or rent a building, owners of real estate and cars, and able to educate their children and have something of their own. The women do not pursue entrepreneurship as an end in itself but as a way of life that helps them manage household poverty and uplift their families. Women were motivated to begin their own businesses by the desire to improve the livelihoods of their family, acquire the best for themselves and liberate themselves from the subordination and control that come with begging for resources or being dependent on somebody else. As one woman trader observed:

> What I have been able to do for my family is the symbol for my entrepreneurial success. Had I sat at home or continued to fight with my husband for not providing, I would not be where I am today. My children tell me that if it were not for my effort, they would not have had an education. They would be taking pails in the morning to milk cows and fetch animal feeds. They would have been hanging out in the village like everyone else. But now, because of me, they have an education and good jobs.
>
> Being independent and shunning from always stretching out my hand to beg from my husband is an indicator of my business success. I am able to pay fees for my child in a private school. I have built my own house and bought a *shamba* [parcel of land]. This has come out of my business. Had I stuck in my miserable job, I would not be where I am.

Independence and flexibility in business are other indicators of entrepreneurial endeavour and success. The women have found an opportunity that releases them from subordinated positions in the households or in their places of work. In the process of making money, the women are transforming themselves into individuals with a voice in their homes. Previously, they were subdued into relying on another person to provide for them or, in the case of the above two responses, they were confined to routine jobs that did not pay well. They have also been able to influence the welfare of the next generation of urban dwellers by providing children with education. This places the children in a better position to manoeuvre and manage life in the city through an intergenerational transfer.

Participating in economic informality creates a sense of control over one's reproductive roles, according to one respondent. This possibility is often not available to women working in regular jobs in the formal sector, since those working in formal jobs have designated time schedules. In economic informality, the time schedules are flexible. As one woman observed:

> I am in control of my life since I have flexible reporting times. I have a small baby who I am breastfeeding. I organize my day's work in a manner that allows me more time to spend with the baby while also giving me time to attend to my business. I could not do the same if I were in an 8 am to 5 pm job.

The allocation of responsibility for fending for the family to the male gender has configured job policies towards the creation of urban jobs for men; the woman is not engaged in production but waits to receive things at home. The women in the study have negated this stereotype of waiting for men to provide for them by starting their own businesses. This running of businesses, they say, comes out of necessity. As one woman noted:

> I have children. I have a desire to see my children succeed. What are they going to eat? These are not the days when women sat passively at home and waited for food and clothing to be brought by someone else. These days call for shared responsibility. The man brings his part and I bring mine. The days of men as sole providers are long gone. Now, men ask what you are also going to offer.

The women's move to bring something to the table challenges the paradigm of the primary male breadwinner in the family. The fact that the women are contributing is in convergence with the traditional African household set-up where the man brought the protein and the woman supplied the grains. In this context, action is required to make the woman's productive environment conducive so that she can share in the responsibility of nurturing. Moreover, the woman does not want to be a mere recipient. While the woman is out to claim active citizenship in the city, it must begin in her home, where she is treated equally both in consumption and in production. In the male breadwinner paradigm of the industrial society, the woman is a consumer and not a producer and therefore she is considered unequal. As one woman trader remarked:

> Let me tell you, I cannot sit and watch my children suffer while I am able-bodied. I have to go and do something outside the home. Times are hard; both

husband and wife have to work to put food on the table. One person's income is not enough. Without an extra income, the family cannot send children to good schools, access medical care, quality food or cater for a wife's needs. It is for this reason that I opened up this stall.

In traditional African logic, a consumer is subordinate to a producer, as expressed in the sayings *mūrūmūrwo ndamenyaga igīthira* (one who is always given does not know when the basket is empty) and *mūheo ndaroga mbūri magego* (a recipient has no choice). The claim for livelihood rights comes from a desire to be a producer in order to supplement incomes, and a desire to improve the lives of the next generation.

Mikell (1997) argues that feminist issues for African women are heterosexual, pro-natal, 'bread and butter' and power issues rather than questions of female control of reproduction, essentialism, the female body or patriarchy discourse. This should not be construed as meaning that African feminism is not concerned about violence associated with sexuality. In the *Agı̃˜ku˜yu˜* context, a woman may be silent about sexuality and birthing, as expressed in the song '*Gu˜ciara gutieri-ragwo gu˜kiragı̃˜rwo ngoro*' ('Birthing and the circumstances surrounding it are not regrettable, but they should remain the secret of my heart'). However, silence does not mean that a woman is not involved in the struggle against sexual subordination. The feminist concerns of women in economic informality go beyond the issues of sexuality to include concerns about the products of sexuality, which entail the continuity of humanity. She acknowledges her sexuality as the link to the continuity of humanity, and the woman's role in this continuity is celebrated. This is expressed in the words of Micere Mugo where she thanks her daughters in the acknowledgements of her book *Writing and Speaking from the Heart of My Mind*: 'no mother could ask for better daughters and I feel extremely fortunate to have these two young women in my life' (Mugo 2012: xii). African women celebrate the continuity of humanity by producing offspring, and they wish their offspring to be better off socioeconomically than themselves. It is for this reason that women engage in productive activities in economic informality. At the height of a woman's transformation and liberation is the struggle not to be in the position of a beggar.

In their desire to bring change to the offspring in their households, women are also generating change in the city. They are making sure that the next generation of city residents is educated and equipped with knowledge. The next generation will be different from the women's own generation, which consisted of migrants from rural areas with little education. They are therefore contributing to the making of the city by investing in human capital and in people who will bring change to the city through knowledge rather than by bootstrap capital like themselves. This resonates with Chant and Pedwell's (2008) recommendations for the need to understand the predominance of women in the informal economy through an analysis of the links between women's productive work and their reproductive work. The women in economic informality celebrate their ability to empower their children by investing in their education, particularly up to university level. As one woman trader attested:

> Through the proceeds of this business, my son has completed his Bachelor of Commerce studies at the University of Nairobi. He is taking additional courses at Strathmore School. He is also helping the business grow since he has more business knowledge than me. While I run the business in an informal way, he is doing it with knowledge and skill. I am happy about it.
>
> This business has done great things for me; I have educated my two children up to university level. My last-born daughter is taking a course at Utalii College. I have also educated my bereaved sister's children to college level; they are all skilled and better suited for jobs in the labour market.
>
> The greatest achievement that I have realized from this business is the education of my children. All my five children have university education. I educated three of them under the parallel programme. What else would I expect in life other than [to] see my children succeed in education and do well?

Needless to say, the future of the cities depends on the quality of human capital in terms of knowledge. This attests to the need to invest in education. The majority of the women in economic informality in the city were migrants with limited education. Their livelihood and citizenship struggle was made difficult by their lack of education and knowledge. Their desire is not to see their children handicapped by a lack of education and therefore they make massive investments in their children's education from their business proceeds. 'My children's education comes first of all my expenses,' said one woman. 'Many people will not understand why I am paying KSh 25,000 for my son's education in kindergarten. It is because I want him to have a good start.'

The women are serving as agents of change for the city residents of the future, since the city itself, with its run-down education infrastructure, is not looking after the transformation of the quality of human capital through education. The women do not want to take chances and so they are enrolling their children in private schools in Nairobi. Three of the five women interviewed had children in private schools, which offer a higher-quality education than the congested city council schools.

Women are actively rescuing the city from the tragedy of intergenerational helplessness and hopelessness by investing in their children and being involved in economic informality. The women entrepreneurs in economic informality are also claiming citizenship in an urban future for their children by investing in human capital through a protracted struggle for livelihoods. They are addressing a critical source of inequality in city education, since education and the right networks ensure that one is able to fit in in the city. They are working against the material deprivation of their children. Rather than modernity occurring through a class struggle that overthrows the dominant classes through insurgency, the women are engaged in an intergeneration change. The next generation will be better equipped to face the future of urban life than the current one. The women are remaking the city by investing in human capital.

Commenting on violence as a means of solving problems or claiming citizenship in the household and in the city, one respondent had this to say:

> Why don't you use the energy to do something different? Why don't you use reason or wisdom-based strategies to do something differently? I am imagining the endless debates going on about poverty; I am imagining the numbers of people who have succumbed to alcoholism and drug addiction due to helplessness and hopelessness and, of course, those who are ready to take up violent means to change the city status quo due to lack of seeing an urban future.

One woman wondered whether this perspective resonates with those regarding the right to the city and the management of urban poverty by saying that:

> I made a decision that rather than spend numerous hours fighting or abusing my husband because of his inability to provide for the family, I would use God-given wisdom. I devised a strategy of using my meagre resources to buy clothes which I would later sell to family and friends to supplement my income. My friend in Thika who was a garment stockist would give me clothes to sell in Nairobi to family and friends. By so doing, I supplemented the family income and did not have to quarrel. This was the humble beginning of my business. This minimized conflicts based on money.

Participation in economic informality is not only about survival, bread and power; it is about knowledge, autonomy and power relationships in the household and in the city. When these issues are dealt with at the household level, they translate spatially to the ward level and eventually to the city. In the eyes of women in economic informality, change in the city begins at the household level. It is where knowledge is created and nurtured and the power balance is generated. By women being actively involved in economic informality, they are able to become active citizens in households and eventually in the city. Thus, as the informal economy transforms, so too are gender and social relationships transformed, and this contributes to the making of the city which in turn makes people. While development practitioners are struggling to rescue women from economic informality, they also need to see the possibility of a city constructed from a platform of economic informality, stable households and human capital.

The entrepreneurial success of women in economic informality is expressed in their act of investing in future human capital. They know that an informed human resource is able to make wise choices. Envisioning an urban future with educated and knowledgeable individuals, the women invest in giving their offspring a good education.

# 7 | The quest for spatial justice: from the margins to the centre

As has been illustrated in the preceding chapters, the city authorities have rarely been supportive of the informal sector. They see it as a nuisance and a source of insecurity. Consecutive local government authorities have therefore worked hard to remove the informal economy from the central business district (CBD), choosing to contain it in the city periphery. The conflict over city space dates back to the colonial period when the city was segregated on the basis of race. During the colonial period, Europeans occupied the most accessible parts of the city while Asians occupied the middle spaces. Africans occupied the city outskirts in the area that is known today as Eastlands. While the African male migrant had the right to access spaces as a worker, the African woman did not have such rights. Her access to the city was determined by marital status.

Historically, women in Kenya were excluded from land ownership in both urban and rural areas by both the patriarchal and the state laws that gave men leverage in land rights. Land belonged to men, and women could have only user rights. However, Kenya's new constitution has given women a reprieve by according them the right to own and inherit land. Land is a critical factor of production: according to Peruvian economist Hernando de Soto, lack of land rights has not only held down the poor of Latin America in informality, but it has also denied them the chance to become capitalists (de Soto 1989). Consequently, the World Bank has proposed the need to ease land rights in developing countries as a strategy to facilitate people's exit from poverty (Deininger 2003).

## Women and land in the city

Production space in Nairobi has largely been determined by an individual's ability to pay for the property. Thus, after independence, buildings that were previously owned by white people were acquired by rich Africans, the majority of whom were men. Ordinary Kenyans could only acquire production spaces by squatting on empty plots, roadsides or undeveloped land (Macharia 1997). A few benefited from the large-scale city council markets such as Quarry Road (Gikomba), Jericho, Uhuru and Kenyatta markets. The initial occupants of these markets were mainly men, but later women gradually gained entry into the markets. The success of women in space acquisition is reflected in the Taveta Road phenomenon, which has seen women acquire most of the shops on the streets and convert them into market exhibition stalls, which they share.

Although the women cross the borders separating their private household spaces from productive spaces, their access to decent lucrative spaces is limited (Table 7.1). Some 21 or 6.5 per cent of the women have acquired business space in the CBD, according to the survey of women in economic informality in Nairobi.

Most of the women in the informal-sector survey are not able to access decent premises to house their businesses (Table 7.2). Of the women surveyed, 116 or 37.2 per cent of them site their businesses in makeshift stalls made of corrugated iron sheets, paper or wood. Only a small proportion of women in the informal economy (85 of 27.2 per cent) house their businesses in permanent stalls, while 27 or 8.7 per cent locate their businesses in commercial buildings. Some 65 or 20.8 per cent house their businesses in open-air markets with sheds constructed

TABLE 7.1  Women's business locations in the city

| Site | Number | Percentage |
| --- | --- | --- |
| Market site | 186 | 57.6 |
| Roadside shoulders | 86 | 26.6 |
| CBD | 21 | 6.5 |
| *Jua kali* site | 18 | 5.6 |
| Empty plot | 6 | 1.9 |
| Residential site | 4 | 1.2 |
| Riverbank | 1 | 0.3 |
| Industrial area | 1 | 0.3 |
| *Total* | 323 | 100 |

TABLE 7.2  Type of women's business buildings in the city

| Type of premises | Number | Percentage |
| --- | --- | --- |
| Makeshift stall (corrugated iron, paper or wood) | 116 | 37.2 |
| Permanent stone stall | 85 | 27.2 |
| Open-air space (paper construction) | 65 | 20.8 |
| Spillover from open-air space (no shed) | 19 | 6.1 |
| Room in commercial building | 27 | 8.7 |
| *Total* | 312 | 100 |

out of polythene paper, while 19 or 6.1 per cent spread their goods on the floor, in spillover areas around open-air markets without sheds.

The women either occupy temporary business premises or have no premises at all; this is an indicator of the discriminatory processes of the largely masculine urban planning ideology that does not consider women as investors or individuals with rights to lucrative urban spaces and premises. It is little wonder then that only 41 or 12.8 per cent of the women intimated that they were allocated business space by the city council of Nairobi.

No fewer than 76 of the informal-sector women (24.1 per cent) own their house of residence. Women who own their own residences make investments in spaces such as Gaberone Road, Dubois Road, Taveta Road, Gikomba, Githurai, Kangemi, Dagoretti Corner, Ngara and Uhuru Market. Some 106 or 33.8 per cent of women in the informal-sector survey indicated that they owned their business premises or stalls. These two categories of women owning stalls and houses are indicative of the positive dynamism that has occurred after women have crossed from their private households into the city. There is also a group of women who have made inroads into the CBD, the majority of whom are concentrated on Taveta Road.

### The Taveta Road phenomenon

Taveta Road is home to 12 buildings, namely Walmart, Jiwabhai Vekaria Building, Midtown Plaza, Merica Plaza, Taveta Court, Annas Centre, ECT Stalls Building, Awas Arcade, Taveta Shopping Mall, Jitihada Shopping Mall and Iqbal Metropolitan Centre. All these buildings are occupied by women who are engaged in selling women's fashion accessories as well as children's clothes. In the 1990s, these buildings housed Asian-owned clothing, housewares and retail shops. One building housed an Uchumi supermarket. Women began the acquisition of this predominantly Asian male productive space by renting a whole shop as a group and subdividing the space into small cubicles or laying out different tables on the shop floor where they spread out their goods, as in the ECT building.

These women are using every opportunity to their own advantage in order to gain entry into the CBD. This positive dynamism inspired by solidarity and improved education illustrates that participation in the informal economy can become transformative and lead to enhanced spatial justice in the city. This kind of spatial justice comes from the grassroots and is well illustrated by the Taveta Road phenomenon in the CBD, where women have acquired regular shops and converted them into informal economy women's business spaces.

Spatial justice for women in Nairobi is envisioned in terms of their right to access spaces of both reproduction and production. During the 1990s, the street was the only space that they could invade and where they could spread their wares. However, in the late 1990s and early 2000s, there was a move to subdivide open-plan shops into stalls or kiosks that could be occupied by micro- and small-scale traders. Ngwala (2011) observes that the subdivision caught planners unawares. The planners could not stop the subdivision as it was happening very quickly, and they were also startled because there were no textbook planning models that could guide them in planning for micro- and small-scale retailers in the city.

Taveta Road can be said to be a female space in the city, constructed by women. The women occupied the street because of the events that took place in the 1990s and 2000s that destabilized the traditional traders in Taveta Road and forced them to move elsewhere. The women at Taveta Road had organized themselves into informal social welfare groups that enabled them to take advantage of the unfolding events in the city as well as solidarity entrepreneurialism.

## Factors that facilitated women's entry into Taveta Road

The space for women's business activities in the centre of town was not handed over to the women on a silver platter. They worked hard for it, aided by solidarity entrepreneurship that hinged on nested communities that were linked by kinship, the same religion, the same lines of business, and friendship. The process was aided by other factors, which included the competition generated by the informal economy, and especially hawkers, that led to the collapse of Asian merchants' businesses. Asian businesses could not survive the competition and were thus forced to exit the market, leaving behind empty buildings in the CBD. Landlords began to subdivide their buildings into small cubicles that could be occupied by former street hawkers. By so doing, the landlords were regularizing the informal economy that for a long time had been a menace to urban planners. In a way, this contributed to the informal economy's grand march from the margins to the centre of the city.

According to a key informant, the liberalization of the housing market in the city led to the rising cost of buildings and premises. As the cost of buildings in the city doubled or tripled, it became difficult for an individual to rent an entire building and make a profit. Asians began to close their shops within the city due to the increased rental costs and the stiff competition their goods were facing from imported items because of trade liberalization. The imported goods were perceived to be of high quality and relatively cheap compared with those produced locally. Furthermore, the merchants were not able to compete with other traders whose transaction costs were greatly reduced because of sharing spaces. In other cases, some prominent businessmen and -women rented the shops and subdivided them into stalls and rented them out to small-scale vendors. These new shop owners seemed to be aware of the high demand for small spaces in Nairobi arising from the expansion of the informal economy, especially from hawkers. Upon subdivision, a regular shop could hold between 15 and 20 cubicles.

The second event was the opening up of new markets for imported goods from China, Dubai, Turkey and South Africa. Travel to these countries was easier than to Europe and North America, which both had stringent visa regulations. Although liberalization led to the closure of businesses, it opened up avenues for new traders who could travel to China, Dubai, Turkey and Thailand in groups. Upon their return, the groups would sell their goods in exhibitions. Initially, customers paid to enter these exhibitions, but this idea was abandoned. At the same time, a new category of women informal traders emerged, made up of women who had been made redundant from their jobs due to the rationalization of the civil service and the closure of factories. These women found the small stalls a positive alternative for doing business.

As mentioned earlier, Mr Nelson Kajuma's 'free market stalls' concept was initiated in the city in the 1990s. Kajuma would construct temporary stalls on sites that he leased from the city council and would in turn rent them out to individuals to carry out small businesses. Kajuma's free market stalls were situated in Uhuru Park. Unlike the hawkers, who were engaged in occasional street battles with city council authorities in the city centre, individuals who sold goods on stalls were not harassed by the council. The hawkers in the city quickly realized that they did not need a large space or street in which to sell their goods, but that they could be housed in a small cubicle and operate without harassment by the city council. This concept was a relief to many hawkers who had experienced marked city council hostility and gave them a sense of entitlement to owning business space. Kajuma's idea of trading in small spaces was therefore welcome and attractive to them. The women feminized Kajuma's concept and looked for buildings in the city to hire out and occupy, while more hawkers began seeking buildings for subdivision into small spaces in which each one of them could trade.

The first building that had been hired out by former hawkers was Sunbeam near Gill House, between Tom Mboya Street and Moi Avenue. Unfortunately, Sunbeam had been condemned for demolition and collapsed during the El Niño rains. When Sunbeam collapsed, the hawkers approached the owner and built temporary stalls for themselves. Other people copied the idea and stalls mushroomed all over Nairobi town. Meanwhile, more shop floors were being converted into stalls because there was a great demand for them.

According to another key informant, the entry into Taveta Road is attributable to the overall socioeconomic changes that took place during President Mwai Kibaki's first regime (2002–07). During this period, the economy grew by 7 per cent. This growth was transferred to economic informality. During Kibaki's time in office, tax collection was streamlined and businesses were closely monitored: some businesses that evaded tax closed down. Some of the monetary reforms introduced under structural adjustment began to bear fruit. Government borrowing from local banks was reduced drastically in the 2000s, which forced the banks to turn to ordinary customers and make personal loans easier to obtain. One respondent stated that she was able to obtain a bank loan using the security of her payslip and that she used the loan to travel to Dubai and rent two stalls. Two local banks, Equity Bank and Family Bank, came up with business-friendly packages for small investors, including those from economic informality. Equity Bank made it easy for small customers to open accounts as well as to take out loans. They also began lending to groups. Women could easily open bank accounts and obtain small loans for working capital.

## Individual stories of enterprise

Women with limited resources excluded by planning ideologies and held back by gender responsibilities have been able to infiltrate the city streets and claim them as their own territory. This phenomenon did not happen by chance. It has been an ongoing struggle against gendered material deprivation as well as a protracted battle for women to become incorporated into the modernity and urbanism project.

The women who acquired space in Taveta Road were drawn from different backgrounds in which they were victims of patriarchy or were confined to specific localities in the city or rural areas by the masculine-oriented tenor of city planning ideologies. Some had been hawkers, some were housewives, while others had worked in offices or had already been workers in the informal economy. Others came after graduating from college upon their failure to obtain formal employment. Others started as employees on the stalls in Taveta Road and then started out on their own or were supported by their spouses or relatives to start a business. What these women have in common is self-drive, courage, passion and entrepreneurial prowess. The women started by making small steps and, through determination, persistence and tenacity, they were able to move from peripheral locations within the city, as illustrated by the following case studies. For some, the preparations began in the rural areas. As one woman trader observed:

> Having not performed well in my high school examination, my parents knew that getting me to a teachers' college, secretarial college or nursing college was not possible. Since I had no money to pay for college education, I started growing French beans in the village to raise money. After making enough money, I moved to Nairobi where I worked as a salesgirl selling clothes for my sister. I worked here between 1983 and 1987. The job involved travelling to distant markets in such places as Western Kenya, Rift Valley and Nyanza. Every Monday, I would take a bale of clothes and move to different markets until I sold all of them. In 1988, my sister realized that I could not continue working for her as I was becoming an adult. I needed to have my own business from which I could rear my children now that I was an adult. She gave me KSh 2,500 and I started my business in Jogoo Road Market. This was a lot of money then. I rented a stall at Jogoo Road and also bought textile material and hired a tailor. I continued going to the market as I did while working

for my sister. My business was booming but in 1989 I decided to move to Gikomba, where I started trading in second-hand clothes. Trade in second-hand clothes was doing very well then. I also joined three *vyama* with other second-hand clothes traders. In 2000, I moved to Kariobangi Market where I made new clothes and also sold materials. I did good business and managed to buy my own stall. In 2003, I decided to leave Kariobangi for the town centre since I learned that Asians were leaving their shops and tenants were subdividing them. I was able to raise money for goodwill from my Kariobangi business and buy this space. In the early days of my life, I had learned that one works hard for others who include family or older siblings. I have learned the importance of investment for myself not just for survival but also to make money. I have learned that I can build a business empire from scratch. I realized from the word go that my engagement in business is not a dress rehearsal. I am putting all my energies in it. I also did not confine myself to one given space. I moved to different spaces.

This illustrates the need for crossing boundaries and making physical movement in the city in search of more lucrative spaces. She gave new meaning to work: she was not just working for survival; she worked hard to grow her business, expand, and reach a level where she could nurture others.

The following case study illustrates another woman's efforts to overcome spatial barriers by physically moving her business:

I had one foot in employment as a nurse and another in *jua kali* [the local name for informal businesses]. My *jua kali* business included upholstery embroidery in a shop in Kayole. In 2002, I decided to relocate my business activity to Ngara Market, which was near the city centre. In Ngara, I engaged in the sale of textile materials and dressmaking accessories such as zips and buttons. Within one year, I was able to purchase a stall, thus stopped renting. As the business continued to boom in 2006, I bought a second stall. In 2007, I learned about vacant business spaces in the town centre. I decided to move into the city and situated my business on the first floor of a building. I did not stop there; in 2008, I moved from the first floor of the building to the ground floor as this was a more accessible place to customers. I also decided to concentrate on selling dressmaking accessories including threads, buttons, zippers, elastics.

Like the above case study, the woman in question realized the importance of making choices between different spaces in the city. In Kayole, her business was situated close to home and rent was cheap, but customers were limited to only those people who lived in the low-income estates. She decided to move into Ngara Market, one of the designated spaces for small-scale traders. However, she did not let this space define her business endeavours and decided to move into the town centre where there were more customers and the space for doing business was strategically situated. This underscores the importance of mobility in business growth. One does not have to be rooted in one space: there are gains for both the business and the person making the physical movement. These two case studies show that women can defy the rule of being physically confined to specific places by their gender or by the physical planning ideologies that locate small traders' markets outside the spaces of action in the city. These women, out of their own determination and tenacity, have not only given a new meaning to women's work but have also illustrated that women can work in and accumulate wealth from big business. They can go beyond survival or 'bread and butter' concerns. They have also realized that different spaces in the city have varying business potential and that this potential can be tapped only through physical movement. Otherwise, they could have just been content in the markets where everybody else was situated.

Another woman, who had been in Taveta Road for a period of nine years after redundancy, had the following to say:

> I have been here for nine years. I was working with the Kenya Post Office until I was retrenched. When I was given my retrenchment benefits, my friend who owned a shop in Moi Avenue and had moved to Taveta Road learned that I was retrenched. She advised me to rent a stall at Taveta Road and promised to accompany me to Turkey or Dubai and show me where to buy goods. We went to Turkey and I came back with a full container of ladieswear. She helped me to sell them. Within two months, the stock was over and I travelled to Turkey, but this time alone.

The essence of the solidarity spirit in this case begins with the altruistic concern of a friend for someone who has been made redundant. She freely gives advice, offers to help, and accompanies the individual to Turkey. She basically initiates her in informal trade after she has left her office job. This is the spirit of ubuntu – 'I am because we are and since we are, I am' (Mbiti 1969: 108). The two women have a vision of growing together towards a future of enhanced prosperity. The future is shared. After initiation by her trade mentor, she begins to work alone. Solidarity here is therefore not geared towards some form of socialism but shared interdependence whereby different individuals provide social infrastructure for each other to survive or derive a livelihood. In this case, the social infrastructure is the embryo for a solidarity that serves as a basis for an individual being initiated into the trade, acquiring space and being helped to market goods.

The women drew support from diverse sources, with some being supported by friends, sisters or spouses, as illustrated in the following case studies:

> I was a housewife and my husband owned a hardware shop at River Road. When we learned that there were stalls opening up at Taveta Road, my husband took a loan from Family Bank. We rented a stall. The money I had was not enough to take me to Turkey or Dubai, pay the rent and buy clothes, so I

took a loan from a *chama* we had formed in 1999. My sister-in-law had already opened her stall and we travelled to Turkey.

The Taveta Road phenomenon has brought visibility to women who had been forced to retreat into the peripheral parts of the city, for example Kamukunji, by the city authorities' anti-hawkers policy. These women experienced different levels of marginalization, as indicated by the following stories:

> I was a hawker. When the police started harassing us, I rented a small room at Kamukunji and started selling household utensils. I had joined two *vyama* which enabled me to start that business. A friend advised me to start saving with Equity Bank and after two years I took a loan of KSh 500,000 from the bank. I rented a stall at Taveta Road and went with my sister, who had already opened her stall at Taveta, to Dubai.

> My husband is a doctor at Kenyatta National Hospital. I was a housewife when in 2007 he took a loan from his Sacco [savings and credit cooperative society] and gave it to me to start the business. A friend of mine who already had opened two stalls at Taveta Road helped me to get a stall and we went together to Turkey and later Dubai. There are many customers here, especially over the weekend and Christmas. Women help one another as you can send a friend going to Turkey or any country to purchase goods.

> After completing my diploma studies in pharmacy, I was frustrated by the amount of money I was getting from my employer. My aunt owned a stall at Sunbeam and she employed me. I was keen to learn the business and when stalls opened up at Taveta Road I approached a friend of my aunt and she employed me. My sister gave me money to rent a stall which I used to sell second-hand clothes. As my business grew, I was able to travel to Turkey or send a friend. The advantage of owning a shop here is that it is well known for the latest fashions and ladies can buy assorted goods. It is a one-stop shopping place where we share ideas.

The case studies illustrate that women came from different backgrounds. They came from the margins of economic informality or were unemployed and constituted a new form of economic informality in the city. They were prompted by the desire to move to the centre of activities. Through individual effort, determination, perseverance and tenacity, they have overcome the conditions of marginalization. Equally important in the movement from the margin to the centre is the support offered by sisters, friends and spouses.

## Solidarity entrepreneurialism

Initiatives at the macro level trickled down to women in economic informality because they already had a social infrastructure, which facilitated business growth and expansion during difficult times. This social infrastructure, locally known as a *chama*, served as the foundation for women in the informal sector to organize themselves. This self-organization enabled them to tap into the benefits of the changes that were taking place nationally. They embraced solidarity entrepreneurialism whereby individuals make investments and share transactions in collaboration with others. They share business information, ideas and space and also undertake joint action in order to reduce transaction costs on transport, rent and information gathering. In addition, they support each other financially.

Solidarity entrepreneurialism has also played a critical role in the movement of women from the margins to the centre in their quest for spatial justice. In groups, the women occupy shop floors and set up garment markets. They also share small spaces situated in open-plan shops. They share space pragmatically without fearing competition, seeing the sharing of spaces through group occupancy as providing more gains than losses. This sharing of spaces not only reduces transaction costs but also bonds them together.

In solidarity entrepreneurialism, the women share and support each other in the ubuntu spirit of 'I am because we are and since we are, I am.' They pool a certain amount of money every day which they give to one person on a rotational basis to buy durable goods or to invest in the business. This enhances their role in production and they have thereby domesticated the microfinance concept of lending. The difference between *chama* lending and that of microfinance is that in the former interest rates are low and loan amounts depend on members' needs, while, in terms of repayment, one can repay the loan with interest as soon as one has completed paying for the transaction for which the loan was intended. The *chama* loans are customized to the needs of women in economic informality.

Solidarity entrepreneurialism based on an extensive use of social capital is an important factor that contributed to the evolution of the Taveta Road phenomenon. One respondent described how she and her friend were working in a clothes shop in Kamukunji, where they pooled their earnings with a view to starting their own business. After accumulating money for three years, they learned about a women's microfinance institution and approached it for funds. They also learned from a friend that business tables were being hired out at Taveta Road. They rented one table and visited a clothing wholesaler at Kamukunji to purchase women's attire for sale. They made good sales but they later decided to trade in children's clothes since everyone on Taveta Road was selling women's clothes.

Trust was also key to the evolution of women's solidarity entrepreneurialism: the women exhibit a degree of trust in each other. At the time of entry, some women already know each other, but a trusting relationship is grown both on the shopfloor and outside the shop (Kinyanjui 2008a). Home visits and the sharing of meals among the women are carried out for bonding purposes, which increases trust. A group can send one person, for example, to Turkey or Tanzania to buy commodities on behalf of the rest. This high degree of trust is exhibited by the fact that the women contribute money to the group, which is later given to one of the members; the women remain part of the group and owe allegiance to it until everybody in the group has received her share, which is another indicator of the high level of trust. Each person on a stall has a person of reference who brought or introduced her to the stalls. So, if someone defaults, her contacts can easily trace her. There are also gatekeepers who keep individuals away who are likely to interfere with the group dynamics. This makes the network of trust complex to outsiders, and if a woman does not know somebody within the group or *chama*, it is not easy to join. It is also difficult to exit because there is peer pressure to stay on. Members draw positive energy from each other.

Solidarity entrepreneurialism also involves collaboration and completion. Much as the women are competitors, selling similar items, they also collaborate in many aspects. The fact that most of the women traders knew each other before they started their businesses in the CBD is the basis of collaboration. One of the areas in which the women show solidarity is the pricing of goods: despite selling similar items, they do not undercut each other and so prices are almost uniform although the items are being sold by different traders. This is a protective measure that ensures that the women traders remain in business. If one sells at lower prices, she is accused of spoiling the market.

Another area where the traders collaborate is in sharing ideas about social and business issues. While waiting for customers, the traders engage in discussions that help them learn from each other. Their discussions include politics and policy issues, and new sources of garments and accessories. Narratives relating to business success are also provided.

Some women also collaborate on international travel. A group may choose to send one person to, for example, Istanbul or Bangkok. This saves travel costs, as the hotel and transport bills are shared, and in turn reduces the prices of commodities. In this way, the women work together as business partners. They also motivate and encourage each other to continue in their businesses. They not only grow together but also empower each other daily.

The women share in the payments for rent, security and water. They also build new relationships: sharing the same building creates the foundations for multiple relationships between the traders and will serve as the basis for further action as well as for the evolution of some kind of agglomeration economies in the locality.

Sharing the same business space has helped the women achieve a level of solidarity that enables them to work out strategies for moving towards a future of prosperity. Through solidarity entrepreneurialism, the women have learned from each other and have contributed to the construction of alternative business spaces. Today, a good number of regular shops on Moi Avenue, Tom Mboya Street, Latema Road and Taveta Road have been converted into small cubicles for trade in clothing and electronics. This is changing the cityscape in this part of town, leading to the emergence of new social alliances among the traders.

Women are therefore helping in the reconfiguration of the city and the construction of a feminine space in the city. The women have made a contribution to the making of the city by using individual and solidarity entrepreneurialism. They are creating a sustainable, equal and liveable space by combining their own labour and capital as well as drawing on their personal networks. The women have become a force in their own right, and this has enabled them to move from obscurity to visibility. According to these case studies, Taveta Road is well known to customers for its women's clothing and accessories and attracts a wide clientele. High-income people can also access it without fear because it is close to the city centre – even prominent people in Kenya visit the area to purchase goods because they know that it is a place where quality clothes from Dubai, Turkey and other countries can be found. The congregation of women selling women's clothes and accessories in one street has contributed to the emergence of an agglomeration of economies. These women have also contributed to the development of a community economy characterized by collaboration. Further, they sell goods without undercutting each other to ensure good neighbourliness.

This analysis of the quest for spatial justice has illustrated that women in the informal economy have been able to carve out a space in the city through individual effort and solidarity entrepreneurialism. The women have established businesses for themselves in legitimate spaces where they do not have to worry about eviction or even garbage collection. By feminizing Kajuma's idea, the women have brought the African indigenous market concept to the CBD and have contributed to the transformation of the cityscape in Taveta Road and in other parts of the city.

# 8 | Women's collective organizations and economic informality

Involvement in the urbanism project in African cities is both an individual issue and a collective one. As individuals migrate into the city, they need to relate to the rest of the people in a community. Often migrants follow or are invited to the city by someone they know, and recent migrants settle and work close to the individuals with whom they are familiar. These relationships are structured into collective organizations or alliances that are formed by migrants from the same rural origin, ethnicity, school, religion, residential area, gender, trade or business sector. The migrants thereby constitute collective organizations through which they communicate and strategize on matters of socioeconomic and political welfare; these associations are part of a large majority of ordinary people's social structure in cities and play important roles in livelihood negotiation (Kinyanjui 2012; Simone 2001a). This chapter presents information on the nature and functions of women's collective organizations in economic informality in Nairobi. However, the focus of this chapter is on the self-organization of women in economic informality, not on externally generated organization. This is the kind of self-organization that emerges from the fact that people with similar norms organize and sustain cooperation that advances their common interests (Ostrom 1990). In the Kenyan African context, such self-organization is based on the principle of 'I am because we are and since we are, I am' (Mbiti 1969: 108). This principle, which is known in South Africa as *ubuntu*, is the basis of social bonding that leads to solidarity and interdependence between people in social and economic action. These collective organizations in Kenya, which are known locally as *chama* (or *vyama* in the plural), have evolved from the traditional African concept of collective organization social groups; these were known as *ngwatio* in Gĩkũyũ, in the case of work and social groups, or *matega* in the case of groups providing mutual assistance during times of illness, childbirth or weddings. The groups were based on friendship or kinship and functioned as work parties that provided labour during tilling and harvesting (Oduol and Kabira 1995). Thus, the current organizations are based on an indigenous African tradition whereby women cooperated and mobilized themselves to assist one another through self-help groups (Oduol and Kabira 1995). Women in economic informality have preserved this cultural concept of solidarity in their urban settings; they have urbanized the concept and used it as a strategy for social and economic support and for coordinating markets and organizing themselves (Kinyanjui 2012). Women in economic informality are therefore offering a link between the past and the present and have created a process of consciously selecting positive cultural traits and adapting them to meet new challenges (Maina-Ahlberg 1991).

The role and the nature of collective organization in economic informality are contested terrains in literature. A strand of literature acknowledges the existence of collective organizations in economic informality (Kinyanjui 2010; Lindell 2010a; Lindell 2010b; Macharia 1997; Meagher 2010) but is divided into two: one strand points to the negative role of collective organizations, while the other focuses on the positive.

One strand of the literature highlights the negative role of collective organizations and strong social bonding in Africa. This strand argues that the demise of the African state, along with the increase in corruption and crime, is due to the strong bonds of client–patron relationships (Bayart 1999; Hyden 1983; Meagher 2010, 2011). Indeed, according to Meagher (2011), social capital among informal workers does not improve popular political representation or governance outcomes in the context of decentralization. In some cases, informal organizations have turned into gangs, such as the case of the Bakassi Boys documented by Meagher (2010). To say the least, collective organizations or networks in some parts of Africa are not developmental. They are embedded in the culture and embroiled in poverty and economic marginalization, making it difficult for them to become competitive or to drive economic dynamism in terms of inter-firm relationships, business growth and export orientation of the economy, like the example of Confucian ethics that has led to the emergence of China as a world powerhouse (Meagher 2012).

The failure of African collective organizations to develop dynamic enterprise clusters similar to the industrial districts in Italy has also been documented. Schmitz and Nadvi (1999) and McCormick (1999) observe that African collective organizations in clusters have failed to generate a collective efficiency that would lead to vibrant industrialization. Thus, while collective action leads to dynamism in other parts of the world (as with Confucian ethics among the Chinese), the African ethic in social networks does not achieve similar outcomes (Meagher 2012). This is because the social capital in African networks is imbued with a spirit of criminality (Meagher 2010) and corruption (Hyden 1983). African networks fail in development terms because of their tendency to concentrate on wealth redistribution rather than on mass wealth accumulation (Chabal and Daloz 1999). These commentators tend to show that African culture and the emerging collective alliances are not developmental.

This chapter is informed by the works of Bourdieu (1986), Coleman (1988) and Ostrom (1990), who demonstrate the value of social capital enshrined in norms, trust and associations in social and economic action in society. These theoretical propositions are supported by empirical studies that have shown that indigenous associations have been useful in forest conservation in the Philippines (Dahal and Adhikari 2008), the management of agricultural markets (Oxfam 2012), infrastructure development in south-western Nigeria (Akinola 2007) and market coordination and social organization in Kenya (Kinyanjui 2012). In particular, strong social bonding characterized by trust and associations has contributed to residents' civic action in eight neighbourhoods in Phoenix, Arizona (Larsen et al. 2004), while collective action has been the basis of insurgent planning that has challenged hegemonic strategies in Cape Town, South Africa (Miraftab 2009).

More evidence of the role of collective organizations in development is appearing in literature (Macharia 1997; Maina-Ahlberg 1991; Berrou and Combarnous 2012; Kebede and Butterfield 2009; Kinyanjui 2012; Lindell 2010a; Lindell 2010b; Stamp 1986). These authors have attempted to show that collective organizations are developmental and have positive roles in society, and especially in the economy. Stamp (1986) describes women's self-help groups as the epicentres of radical consciousness in the countryside. The women not only use them to resist but also for self-transformation. Maina-Ahlberg (1991) illustrates the important role of women's mutual support groups in regulating sex and reproductive health in central Kenya. She illustrates how the groups have helped women learn about the need for spacing children by encouraging them to accept contraception. The groups were also involved in economic activities and created agency that gave women confidence to attempt changes or resist changes in ways that an individual woman cannot do. Donaldson (1997) has shown that Tshunyane women in South Africa turn to family networks in order to make critical decisions concerning their health and the health of young children in their care.

Social networks based on friendship and kinship have been documented as constituting an important social and political dynamic of the informal economy in Harare and Nairobi (Macharia 1997). Social networks were important in skills training, migration and business start-ups, as well as in giving advice to entrepreneurs. Macharia also observed that women's social networks were growing despite the lack of government support. Women tended to establish close co-ethnic networks that provided emotional support and rotational credit services. These functions were important for the survival of women's businesses.

Berrou and Combarnous (2012) have shown that the personal networks of entrepreneurs play an important role in the informal African economy. The strong ties provide a basis for the efficient circulation of resources and facilitate entrepreneurs' access to information, financial support and business partnership. They also play a significant role in informal social insurance and accessibility to market resources. Thus, strong ties have a positive impact on informal urban economies because they reduce transactional costs. The importance of social networks, especially among poor women, has been documented in Ethiopia (Kebede and Butterfield 2009), where networks based on ethnicity, trust, kinship and marital status, among other factors, play a key role in community development. These authors further show that the traditional *iddir* and *iqqub* organizations influence the socioeconomic context of the poor.

Collective organizations play an important part in some forms of informal economy, particularly in scaling up, by potentially opening up new possibilities for political intervention (Lindell 2010b). This new role is creating a new dimension of collective organization that is different from the previously inward-looking associations that mainly subscribed to welfare activities (McCormick et al. 2003; Mitullah 2003).

My previous work has shown that there are several types of *vyama* that have different functions and roles in the community. They are important in facilitating ordinary people's market coordination and society organizations; they have been avenues not only for redistribution but also for wealth accumulation and investment; and they have also been important in providing social insurance as well as vehicles for accessing work. Undoubtedly, the *vyama* have had a positive impact on ordinary people's identity construction and exit from marginalization.

Informal economy workers, especially women, have support organizations that are used to coordinate their affairs in the city, although these organizations are invisible to the government and below the development practitioners' radar. Despite the marginalization of collective organizations among people in economic informality in both urban studies scholarship and planning, people are important in urban Africa. Simone's (2004) perception of people as infrastructure assumes that they constitute the frame upon which social and economic action is constructed in African cities. It is impossible to imagine what conditions in economic informality would be like if there were no collective organizations to regulate them. Simone's notion of people as infrastructure in African cities can only work if there are collective organizations coordinating people's activities. It is also unlikely that individuals who live and work in close proximity to each other would lack some form of collective organization.

Informal workers in the city, and especially women, are collectively organized in *vyama*. These *vyama* are used to drive social and economic action. According to the case study focusing on Taveta Road's women traders, women join these collective organizations for solidarity, 'to work together with others': 'One cannot just work alone, one needs others to work with,' observed a member of one of the women's groups. They also join collective organizations in order to have an identity as well as to become a member of a community. 'The *chama* gives me a sense of belonging to a community. It gives me confidence to do business as well as live in the city,' stated another. 'The *chama* sustains me. I get lump sum money when it is my turn or I borrow money at low interest rates.' 'It builds my ability to engage in everyday life,' asserted another woman. Essentially, the *chama* is an investment in social capital and solidarity that improves the capability of women to engage in the modernity and urbanization project in the city. Individually, the women would be constrained or lack the energy to engage, but through the *chama* they are able to become social actors in their own transformation in the city.

### The street or market collective organization (*chama cha soko*)

The collective organization of women in economic informality is on two levels. The first level involves membership of the *chama cha soko* (the street or market association) while the second level involves membership of smaller *vyama* organizations. The *chama cha soko* collective organization in Nairobi is somewhat similar to other economic informality associations, such as those found in Aba manufacturing clusters in Nigeria (Meagher 2010) or market associations in Ghana (Clark 2010). The *chama cha soko* enlists membership from all the women involved in the market, for example those in the ECT Building and Jitihada Shopping Mall on Taveta Road, Cianda Market along Nairobi's Ronald Ngala Street, or Stage Market. Every woman is supposed to make daily contributions to the *chama cha soko*; the purpose of these contributions is to take care of security, to ensure that the business premises are kept clean, to coordinate the affairs of the traders, settle disputes, and control the opening and closing times of the business premises.

The *chama cha soko* serves as the link between the traders and the city council. For example, if city rates are being revised by the council authorities, the information is communicated to the leadership who in turn negotiate with the council authorities when necessary. They use their collective effort to challenge council fees and regulations. If the members have complaints about the markets, the chairperson communicates with the council or the landlord of the building or stall. In some instances, new members have to be cleared by the *chama cha soko*. All in all, the *chama cha soko* maintains law, order and the smooth running of market affairs.

The affairs of the *chama cha soko* are managed by a body of elected leaders comprising the chairperson, secretary, treasurer and their deputies as well as committee members. It is governed by a constitution that defines rules and regulations for managing traders. The leadership plays an important role in dispute resolution: if members have problems with one another, the first person to go to is one of the leaders of the *chama cha soko*. In some large markets, the *chama cha soko* provides savings and credit services to its members.

Although it may appear that the *chama cha soko* does not engage in open and active politics, its role is important in representing the interests of the traders in the city. For example, when Uhuru Market stalls were burned down, the *chama* lobbied the city council of Nairobi and the constituency development fund to build modern stalls. In Taveta Road, the *chama cha soko* ensures that rents are not hiked and handles the council inspectors. It also encourages its members to comply with regulations such as the buying of business permits so that the shared shop is not closed.

The *chama cha soko* is unlike the informal economy associations in Latin America and South Africa that actively resist government plans, especially when they act to the detriment of the informal economy (Hlela 2003; Lazar 2007). The *chama cha soko* regulates businesses that are in legitimate spaces in the city, such as shops and markets. Points of conflict with the council authorities arise in matters relating to rates, parking fees for goods freighters and payment for licences. A case in point is when micro-retailers occupied one shop and proposed to pay a single licence that would cover all the occupants, whereas the council demanded that each of the tenants in the building should hold a licence and pay for it. Negotiations between the council and representatives of the micro-retailers were initiated and are still ongoing at the time of writing. The traders make extensive use of social capital, raising the alarm over different issues and incidents. Once such alarms are raised, people crowd round and surround the area immediately, ready to rescue their comrades.

Informal businesses form and evolve beyond state regulation, as observed by Lindell (2010b); this could constitute a form of the informal economy's subliminal resistance to organization by the state. However, the *chama cha soko* becomes the infrastructure for monitoring the state. Every change in policy or management personnel in the city administration is studied and analysed to ascertain what precautions or actions should be taken. The *chama cha soko* ensures that the interests of the traders are not sidelined in social and political changes. When need arises, the *chama cha soko* mobilizes its members to take political action; if that action means resistance, participation, collaboration or partnership, members are mobilized accordingly.

The *chama cha soko* also ensures that the economic informality subculture in the city is maintained and not lost. This may sound strange, but some benefits can accrue from operating in this subculture, safeguarded by city council by-laws. For example, individuals operating in temporary situations or in markets are exempt from tax; as a result, they are not encouraged to register their businesses and therefore they can trade anonymously (Kinyanjui 2010).

Membership of the *chama cha soko* legitimizes one's operation in the market and enhances one's latitude of operation in the city. It also gives people an identity as a market trader. Market traders are resilient, entrepreneurial, confident and aggressive. They are known for their shrewdness. The market association acts as the guardian of these identities. For example, if one trader decides to flout the pricing rules, the individual is isolated and can even be expelled from the market. The discourse and lingua franca in the *chama cha soko* is one of toughness. If someone breaks the rules, that person is subjected to what is known in Gĩkũyũ parlance as *kũhandwa* (being brought down to ground level).

## Characteristics of women's collective organizations (*vyama*)

The second type of collective organization is the *chama* or *vyama* of friends, women in the same line of business or those sharing the same buildings. This type of *chama* is a membership organization bringing together different women into a social group. A woman can belong to many *vyama* involving different people. The fundamental principle of *vyama* membership is that women in the informal sector realize that they cannot survive as individual, atomistic traders in an otherwise hostile and uncertain environment. Survival and business growth hinge on a myriad of everyday interactions that range from the exchange of ideas in informal chats to monetary and business support. The women have moved a step further and have formalized their relationships with each other by forming social groups locally known as *vyama.*

According to the survey carried out, the duration of membership of a *chama* ranged between two months and ten years. Some women belonged to as many as five *vyama.* Some groups may have as few as five people while others may have as many as a hundred women. The *chama* has defined rules and regulations and the members are required to make specific contributions of money, which can be daily, weekly, fortnightly or monthly. The monetary contribution to the *chama* could be as low as KSh 50 per day and as high as KSh 10,000 per month, depending on the income levels of the group's members. The groups have a variety of names that express their philosophies and functions.

*The role of* vyama  Table 8.1 presents *chama* names put forward during the sample survey of women in economic informality. Five groups had English names, two had Gĩkũyũ names, while the rest had Swahili names. Five major themes were discerned from the *chama* names: unity, identity, self-help, friendship and individual progress. These themes were based on what the names literally mean. There are also groups organized by non-governmental organizations (NGOs) and groups named after places.

The names given to the diverse groups reflect their purpose. The most common theme emerging from the group names is the need for women to work together as they address their socioeconomic marginalization. This theme also gives an indication of the need for women to interact and chart their destiny together, or the need for them to share experiences. The theme relating to having a women's identity emphasizes the need for women to recognize their worth and use this worth to navigate marginalization: that is, they should mark their boundaries and be able to stand up for their rights. This could be another innovation: the women in the informal economy are domesticating the rights awareness campaigns that are ongoing in the country. The other theme that emerges from the names is the need for women to develop themselves. They are acknowledging that they are not able to address their socioeconomic and political challenges if they are not empowered, or if they do not have the capacity to do so. It

TABLE 8.1 *Chama* names and themes

| Name | Theme |
| --- | --- |
| Africa Share Partnership | Unity, benevolence |
| Muungano Wetu | Unity |
| Muruna | Comradeship, friendship |
| Pamoja Women's Self-Help | Togetherness, self-help |
| Simama | Identity, proactivity |
| United Women's Group | Unity |
| Elite | Uniqueness, specialness |
| Kenya Mpya Women's Group | Newness |
| Mapato Savings Group | Saving |
| Merry-Go-Round | Rotational savings |
| Kamati ya Wanawake Chipukizi | Unity |
| Witeithie Women's Group | Self-help |
| Kariobangi Women's Group | Place |
| Wanawake Tujijenge | Individual progress |
| Umoja Business Women's Group | Togetherness |
| Dandora Self-Help | Place |
| PAWDEP Thika | NGO |
| Green Apple | Fruit |

*Source*: Author's survey, 2012.

is only by building this capacity that they are able to work together and to help their needy members too. Friendship also emerges as a theme in the names of women's groups; this emphasizes the need for a shared destiny and calls upon the women to be supportive of each other. The self-development or 'help yourself' theme implies that, for any change in society to occur, it must start with individuals. It is their responsibility to carry out transformation among themselves in order to realize the individual future that each of them envisions.

The tenets of unity, solidarity, togetherness and comradeship serve as strategies for rescuing women from material deprivation and exclusion from spaces of action. These attributes are essential for building collective agency. Thus, rather than the women exiting or withdrawing due to exclusion, they are ganging up together to face constraints on moving to the centre. This movement is not only in terms of physical mobility from marginal spaces in the urban peripheries, but also refers to personal development. This is because most of the women engaged in economic informality have relatively low levels of education, are recent migrants and, if married, are dependent on their male spouse. Collective agency is therefore required at both the individual level and the group level.

At the individual level, a woman needs to mobilize resources as well as to harness the confidence needed to make a move. Women cannot win the battle against material deprivation and confinement to the margins alone: they need to work together in solidarity to access spaces and overcome resource constraints. As shown in the early chapters, these problems are determined historically and women need concerted efforts to overcome them.

Table 8.2 illustrates the specific functions of the *chama*. The most important function, as indicated by 59 or 36.9 per cent of the respondents in the survey, is to collect money from members and then give some percentage of the money to one of the group members while the rest is saved. This is done on a rotational basis until all members have received their percentage of the money. The next most important function, indicated by 46 or 28.8 per cent of the respondents, is savings and credit. This involves members contributing to a kitty and then lending money to members at a low interest rate. Again, this is done on a rotational basis. Economic empowerment is another important function of the *chama*, cited by 32 or 20.0 per cent of the respondents. This entails making group investments such as buying shares on the stock exchange, buying rental plots or making targeted savings for a particular item. These items can range from foodstuffs and durable household goods to plots of land for constructing rental housing. The next important category is helping the women improve their businesses. This relates to the sourcing of products, where a group of women may sponsor one of the group to travel and make purchases, or encouraging each other to start saving in banks and sharing new techniques of production in the case of manufacturing.

Although most of the *vyama* have social functions, such as celebrating life, helping pay medical bills and funeral support – and six reported that they were formed to carry out such functions – innovative socio-cultural and economic processes have evolved from the associations of women in economic informality, such as visiting parents for *Kamweretho* (to speak out). *Kamweretho* is one of

TABLE 8.2 Specific functions of the *chama*

| Function | No. | Percentage |
| --- | --- | --- |
| Collect and distribute money to one person | 59 | 36.9 |
| Savings and credit | 46 | 28.8 |
| Economic empowerment and social support (funerals, medical bills, etc.) | 32 | 20.0 |
| Improve members' businesses | 17 | 10.6 |
| Social (Kamweretho) | 6 | 3.8 |
| *Total* | 160 | 100 |

the most recent innovations in the social functions of the *chama* among those organizations composed of Agĩkũyũ women (Kinyanjui and Gichuhi 2010). The introduction of *Kamweretho* is innovative in the sense that the women use an indigenous rite to negotiate for women's rights and to resist subordination. This movement enhances women's gender identity and repositions women in the changing socio-cultural environment (Kinyanjui and Gichuhi 2010). *Kamweretho* is a function in which women in a group visit each member's parent to express gratitude and collectively discuss (or speak out on) a number of issues regarding women's rights. For unmarried single parents, it involves paying the bridal wealth (*kwigũra*); when a woman performs this action, it means that she has access to her ancestral land rights and can also receive bride wealth for her children (Kinyanjui and Gichuhi 2010).

The ceremony is also a social legitimization of women as accumulators of capital. After receiving blessings from their respective parents, women who have undergone the ceremony are involved in purchasing land for redistribution to members and buying other assets in the city. The women are therefore moving towards some form of transformation that is sanctioned through indigenous cultural events. They are claiming rights in the city by first dealing with how they are defined and framed at the household level. They recognize that it is important to first resolve cultural expectations and then move on to the next phase of empowerment and liberation.

Whereas cultural rights may be seen as retrogressive in an urban setting, women are adopting some of them in a positive way to lay claim to their rights to the city. The dynamic here is that women in the informal economy have internalized the struggle for women's rights that is going on in the city but they have indigenized it, owned it and given it a mark of ordinariness. It will no longer be unusual for a woman to own land or property in the city; they will have acquired it legitimately. They will not have acquired it through prostitution, as in the songs of popular culture musicians or the writings of Bujra (1975) and White (1990) in their works on early women migrants and prostitution in Nairobi. Women are renegotiating their positions as decent women who acquire wealth through legitimate means in economic informality. They are using the dynamism of the group to realize this objective of negotiating their identity in the city. Women who work together every day in markets are speaking out about their role in the city. The *chama* is therefore playing a pivotal role in the reimagining and packaging of women in the city.

Collective organization is inevitable in economic informality because of the nature of entry and the way in which women stay in business, as well as the nature of coordination of supply and distribution chains. In most instances, an individual is introduced into economic informality by a relative or someone from the same village, residential estate or religion. It is imperative that relationships are maintained. One needs someone to chat with while waiting for customers and someone with whom to share transport costs for freighting goods or security costs for guarding the premises. The small shared spaces also necessitate the maintenance of relationships with fellow traders because the distances between each other are minimal and sometimes there are no walls. Such relationships are woven into collective organizations in order to regularize the daily social and business interactions as well as to overcome constraints encountered in accessing space or doing business.

The desire for relationships and interactions can only be understood within the context of the African principle 'I am because we are and since we are, I am'. This concept has been adopted and extended by Christian churches: one has to belong to a small Christian community in the case of the Catholic church or to a fellowship cluster in Protestant and Pentecostal churches. The need for alliances also arises because of the need for security in residential estates (Kinyanjui 2010).

As the survey revealed, the basis of solidarity was friendship, being in the same line of business, living in the same neighbourhood or sharing a business space. Occupying the same business space seems to be particularly important for a woman's choice of who to relate with. This neighbourhood effect is particularly important in the formation of an informal economy among women entrepreneurs since it determines their modes of interaction. As the women sit together all day over the course of a week, a month and a year, they are bound to influence each other on a range of issues. New bonds emerge and individuals acquire new perspectives about issues as they learn from each other. This in turn creates and supports nested communities that lay claim to spaces in the city, making the city an interconnected whole. For example, if a *chama* member decides to invest in a particular neighbourhood, more often than not other members will follow her. In other instances, a member will take responsibility for inviting others to join her in the spirit of solidarity entrepreneurialism. By so doing, she will be creating another nested community in another space. Spatially, these nested communities contribute to the overall sprawl of informality. This happens so quickly that urban planners are caught unawares (Ngwala 2011).

The occupation of Taveta Road followed the same pattern of individuals inviting others to join them. The stalls were not advertised but they kept on being filled as friends and relatives brought in their friends. This process means that individuals already know each other, and so it is no wonder that as the women sit and wait for customers they chat about experiences or have heated debates on a range of social and economic concerns, from the daily news to politics and business issues. The women discuss issues that affect them as women in the household and in the public domain.

The *chama* is therefore a platform for discussion that helps women negotiate livelihoods in a city where historically they have been outsiders. It serves as the infrastructure for communication and collaboration. With regard to communication, chats, narratives and discussions held between members go beyond groaning and moaning about women's disadvantaged situation and position in the city. The discussions become sources of agency and synergy for improving women's status quo. They not only shape opinions but may have a bearing on the way in which women marketers behave, influencing women's perceptions of business in the market. As one woman trader said:

> I started retailing children's clothes. After a small chat with one woman on
> how much I was making from the children's clothing, the next thing was
> that she also changed into retailing children's clothes. She talked with some
> other three women about it and they also started selling children's clothes.
> With time, everyone here was keeping children's clothes. Our shop now just
> contains children's clothes.

The importance of chatting is echoed in a different context by Simone (2011: 360), who says that:

> it is the basis from which people can speak to various situations on the street,
> bar or office so as to possibly shape the outcome. In this way they do not leave
> themselves vulnerable to the impacts of other people's actions. It provides
> them with a basis to intervene in situations that on the surface would not
> seem to be their business or concern.

The fact that the women discuss a range of social, economic and political concerns helps them go through their day-to-day experiences in the city. They need to know the cost of goods, where to pay licences, where to source supplies, which council department and staff to deal with, which streets are safe, the cheapest mode of travel, where plots are being sold, good schools for their children, where to live, the best doctor to see in the city or the changes that have taken place in the country. This information will help them make informed decisions in business and at the household level. Through chatting, the women mobilize a lot of information that they later synthesize and apply in their livelihood negotiation in the city. The information also helps them construct their identity.

The women in the informal economy are moving from being dependants to accumulators. The movement is not haphazard, as envisioned in the literature on the impact of informality in the city; it is discussed and coordinated. It begins with simple interactions with immediate neighbours in the market space and extends to the *chama*. The *chama* then serves as a space and site for interaction and for strategizing socioeconomic action that has a bearing on the construction of the reality of informality in the city.

Dealing with urban informality does not just mean regularizing land rights, as neoliberals such as Hernando de Soto (1989) would want us to believe; it means dealing with the emergent subcultures that arise from the collective alliances in urban informality. These collective alliances are based on the past, present and imagined futures of the cities and what women would like to be. The subcultures and the collective agency frame and shape the social spatial dynamism of the city. These collective alliances are as dynamic as the people and often leave imprints on the city: for example, when the construction of high-rise gated communities suddenly sprouted in the upper-class neighbourhoods of Nairobi, the concept was quickly picked up by the sprawling informal settlements of Zimmerman, Githurai, Wendani, Mathare North, Kayole and Kahawa Jua Kali. Even in Mathare, along Juja Road, there are some isolated high-rise stone buildings. This is illustrative of the fact that the social spatial frontiers of informality in the city are transforming at a rate which reveals that people are finding more and more new ideas and creating agency to drive them.

The ideas may come from observation, *chama* discussions, the church, movies, the city or the upper-income neighbourhoods where these informal businesses are located. The *chama* enables women to cross borders between the formal and the informal city. When they return from the city centre, the women come with ideas and perceptions of what their surroundings and their houses should be like. The ideas help them create visions and initiate images of what social spatial dynamism should be. Where they can, the women copy their visions of the city; and where they cannot, they substitute them with the past or imagine how things will be in the future.

It is therefore not uncommon to find a market woman's house replete with interior decor made by informal economy manufacturers, or her walls, seats, table or stool covered with cloth upholstery purchased from the second-hand market in Gikomba or made by informal garment makers in Uhuru or Githurai Markets. The house may also have a radio, a television set, a Meko gas stove, which is interchangeable with a kerosene stove, nice serving dishes, and other household utensils bought with proceeds from the *chama*. One might find that a woman in the informal economy who owns a house has constructed some three rooms for her family. She may also have extended her house by building extra rooms for renting out. Some rooms may be complete while others are in the process of construction, because the pace of building work is determined by the way she makes her money. Thus, the woman is not only shaped by informality but also contributes to the shaping of the urban form. She has moved from being a marketer to a property owner and a housing provider in the city.

*Issue management in* vyama Several issues are discussed in *chama* meetings (Table 8.3). The largest number of women's *vyama* (65 or 29.6 per cent) spend time discussing group investments while the second–largest category of *chama* (39 or 17.7 per cent) hold meetings to discuss self-improvement. About 38 or 17.3 per cent hold meetings to discuss social and economic issues affecting the women, while another category of *chama* (30 or 13.6 per cent) hold meetings

TABLE 8.3 Issues discussed in the *chama*

| Issue | No. of vyama | Percentage |
|---|---|---|
| Group investment | 65 | 29.6 |
| How to improve ourselves | 39 | 17.7 |
| Social and economic issues | 38 | 17.3 |
| Business improvement and loan management | 30 | 13.6 |
| Challenges in the business world | 12 | 5.5 |
| How to contribute money | 11 | 5.0 |
| Spiritual matters | 9 | 4.1 |
| Visits to each other | 8 | 3.6 |
| Sharing of income between members | 5 | 2.3 |
| Reducing the number of women in the market | 2 | 0.9 |
| Visits to the less privileged | 1 | 0.5 |
| *Total* | 220 | 100 |

*Source*: Author's survey, 2012.

to discuss business improvement and the management of group loans. About 12 or 5.5 per cent of the *chama* members hold meetings to discuss challenges in business while 11 or 5 per cent talk about how members contribute money. Other issues discussed in meetings include spiritual matters.

This implies that social and economic decisions affecting women in the informal economy are not always taken in a haphazard manner or spontaneously. They are discussed and minutes are recorded and kept by the *chama* secretary. In the meetings, women deliberate on their visions, challenges and strategies to help realize their goals, and they also plan. The *chama* gives the women space and opportunity to discuss issues and approve them for action. It is the new space for women's interaction. This strengthens and concretizes the social forms that constitute the infrastructure on which economic informality thrives. Informality is therefore constructed on group rationality, the logic of which is derived from discussions held in democratic settings rather than from the uncoordinated actions of mobs of women earning a pittance in the city.

This gives the impression that there is 'organized disorder' in economic informality. The kind of organization that exists in informality is reflected in Adichie's description of the market in Kano in her book *Half of a Yellow Sun*:

> On the narrow market paths, she maneuvered between small boys carrying large loads on their heads, women haggling, traders shouting (Adichie 2009: 37).

She pulled down the wooden shutters of the kiosk, covering the neatly arranged cases of matches, chewing gum, sweets, cigarettes, and detergent ... The narrow bungalow was unpainted. The clothes hung out to dry were still stiff as if desiccated by the hot afternoon sun. Old car tyres, the ones the children played with, were piled under the kuka tree (Adichie 2009: 39).

People take time to organize the apparent disorder and some of their efforts in this regard include forming social groups such as the *chama* that bring them together to chart a course for their destiny. Konings et al., quoted in Myers (2011), observe that residents in disadvantaged African neighbourhoods do not just sit and watch situations and conditions deteriorate. They take action and devise strategies that shape their livelihoods. These actions are often not spontaneous; they are discussed both in informal chats and in formal settings such as the *chama*. Decisions are also taken in collective solidarity among the members of the group. The substructures created by the collective solidarity are responsible for the sprawl of informality and its complexity. This is because when action is being taken, there is the individual, the neighbour, the friend and the *chama* that all have to be consulted before changes can be made or before one joins the informal economy. Someone cannot be rejected arbitrarily because she could be a neighbour, a friend or a member of a *chama*. These social arrangements may perhaps explain the sprawl of informality in contemporary African cities, which occurs as a result of collective agency that configures what we see as informality.

Another social innovation is in relation to women's *vyama* adopting the microfinance principle of lending and the group guaranteeing for each other. The domestication of microfinance principles into the local market setting is one area where such associations have been liberative. In addition, women's collective organization has led them to travel abroad to source goods rather than buying from local wholesalers. A *chama* of women may, for example, decide to raise money and travel to Dubai, China or Turkey to buy goods. This ensures that they are able to procure goods from the source without the intervention of middlemen. It also saves costs and ensures that goods and items are priced competitively.

Collective organization has also led to product improvement; women discuss product designs and the latest models on the market both locally and internationally, thereby improving the products they sell. Through collective action, women have also been able to address the challenges of space in the market sites. These challenges could relate to the lack of clean toilets, congestion, the fact that market spaces are not expanded, or the failure to create more markets.

In view of the hardships and uncertainties characterizing economic informality, many individuals would have given up. Group therapy – the fact that the women are all in it together – provides synergy to stay on. The learning that takes place between and among women also improves their capability, while the *chama* inspires collective self-belief among them.

The women support each other in fundraising through their pooled savings. When one of the group members is given a lump sum of money, she is able to add stock, clear debt or pay school fees. The women are also able to borrow money with lower interest rates than those available from banks, moneylenders or microfinance. As the women discuss and tell stories about politicians and their achievements and political scandals in their *chama*, they enhance their political stands on many issues. They enlighten and influence each other so that they construct a politics of women in economic informality. Perhaps this is why markets become important sites for political campaigners during civic and national elections. It is said that market women are important for influencing political opinions, hence the need for politicians to visit them. The women do not protest openly or enter into direct confrontation but their influence is felt in their daily practices, such as the quiet occupation of Taveta Road.

Doing business on a stall or in a kiosk is not the equivalent of poverty. Some of the individuals doing business in markets and on stalls have investments in the emerging settlements of Kayole, Githurai, Mwihoko, Kahawa Jua Kali, Kahawa Wendani, Kasarani, Kawangware, Ngong, Kiserian, Roysambu, Zimmerman and Mlolongo. They also have investments in rural areas. These traders are well connected socially and politically and have a role in the way Nairobi is being constructed and reconstructed. Over time, they have developed a livelihood network in the city that is difficult to penetrate or wish away. There is a need to create places for them in city planning and management committees: this is how an inclusive and integrated city should be realized.

The city knows very well that it gains from economic informality. The city has 2.7 million informal workers, according to the Kenya National Bureau of Statistics. If we assume that each worker pays a daily fee of KSh 30, simple arithmetic tells us that the city makes about KSh 81 million daily from informal workers. If 80 per cent of these informal workers are women, as stated in International Labour Organization statistics, the city is drawing a large amount of money from its women, and this is another reason why it should not wish to see informality eclipsed. Since the city is dependent on economic informality and women as sources of revenue, it has an obligation to agree to include economic informality in its city administration and management organizations through the women's *vyama*. This will involve inviting representatives from economic informality onto committees running the affairs of the city.

The survey and case studies revealed that women are already in groups. This is a good starting point for social and economic action to address spatial justice, mobility and participation in urban development. It is important to build on the existing mechanisms that the women themselves have initiated. After all, the

114

*vyama* have some guiding philosophies and ideologies that can be tapped into. The *chama* is a liberative innovation originated by women and that women join out of their free will. It can therefore be utilized as an organizing principle for women in the city.

This analysis has illustrated that collective organizations in economic informality, especially those relating to women, are developmental. They create spaces of interaction and the negotiation of rights; sources of finance, social insurance and investment; and links with the city council. To argue that these collective organizations are opportunistic is far from the truth. They are based on solidarity and common understanding among individuals who have been historically marginalized into subalternity and who are struggling with the same goal of participating in the modernity and urbanism project.

Stating that collective alliances in economic informality are embedded in retrogressive cultures is apportioning developmental values to some communities and denying others the same. It is the same as assuming that some communities are at the dress rehearsal stage for their livelihoods while others are actually living. Similarly, the attribution of a spirit of criminality to all African collective organizations is far from plausible. There could be criminal elements in some cases but not everyone is a criminal. There are individuals who derive honest livelihoods in economic informality and organize legitimately.

The bottom line in the analysis of collective organization is that subalterns' – and more specifically women's – epistemologies have been subordinated. There is a tendency to privilege some communities' epistemologies, especially those from the West – and now from the East as well – at the expense of African perspectives. It largely remains to be seen whether this positioning of knowledge is by design or by accident.

# 9 | Conclusion

In this book I set out to answer the question of how women have navigated around the various conditions and policies in the city of Nairobi, moving from the margins of the city to the city centre, after decades of exclusion and marginalization. I also set out to discover the various creative methods that women have used in their journey from the margins to the centre. The women have had to traverse the complexity of urbanization characterized by patriarchal planning ideologies, gender inequality and economic informality.

## Complexity of urbanization

The drastic expansion of urbanization over the past four decades has made urbanization one of the defining features of the twentieth and twenty-first centuries. Rapid urbanization, dominant economic informality, gender inequality and the unplanned nature of urban settings characterize most African cities. While urbanization in Africa is experiencing expansion – largely triggered by rural–urban migration and natural population growth rates in cities – it has failed to bring about inclusive growth, leading to the rise of slums and the prevalence of economic informality.

Urbanization is complicated by planning ideologies that exclude rather than include. Nairobi city was never really meant for all. In particular, the planning ideologies to a large extent exclude women and individuals involved in economic informality. An analysis of the historical evolution of Nairobi reveals that the city had restrictions and boundaries created to control the location and situation of people on the basis of race, ethnicity and gender. This segregation determined where one could live and work. The historical analysis further demonstrates how planners struggled to address the problems of segregated cities in the first and second decades after independence, and that any momentum was lost in the subsequent planning decades. To a great extent this historical factor has had a bearing on the nature of the socioeconomic development movements that have been going on in the city in terms of spatial justice for different categories of people but particularly for women, who were historically disadvantaged in terms of migration and urbanization.

## Economic informality

Although there has been a hostile attitude towards economic informality, it is at the core of the formation of African cities. In the 1990s, Nairobi's economy faced significant challenges attributable to the structural adjustment programmes dictated by the Bretton Woods institutions. The restructuring produced widespread public-sector job losses, an increase in the number of unemployed school and college graduates, a lack of quality and dependable jobs, the collapse of industries, and a lack of coordination between the Ministry of Local Government and the Ministry of Trade. The city's formal economy stagnated as informal and unregulated activities flourished. Opening up to the global economy initially resulted in declining living standards, growing inequality and division. This was further exacerbated by the arrival of growing numbers of people who were fleeing the violence in Somalia, Rwanda and Burundi. As expressed in the earlier chapters, most of the people in economic informality were labelled a security risk and were consequently harassed by the central government in the 1990s when the city administration was run by individuals affiliated to the parties in opposition. The government was keen to keep the opposition from infiltrating the volatile groups of hawkers.

Local and national government used a mix of policies, for example licensing, the African indigenous market concept, *turudi mashambani* (encouraging urban–rural migration) and demolitions. It was feared that if the hawkers became economically powerful, they would threaten the existing power hegemony in the city. Successive governments have not fared any better. They have manipulated economic informality operators to suit their political whims and have discarded them when they become inconvenient.

In 1993, 'The Nairobi We Want' campaign sought to address quality-of-life issues under the leadership of Mayor Steve Mwangi, as the city council returned to the forefront of the urban governance matrix. The campaign initiated local government reforms and saw the city embrace public–private partnerships such as the Nairobi Central Business District Association for infrastructure development, service delivery and investment revenue.

In the dualist and structuralist models of economic informality, it was argued that the informal sector would disappear in African economies once the survivalists' tendencies were catered for through modernization and formalization. Forty years down the line, however, the informal sector is still resilient. Successful corporations such as Safaricom (a mobile telephony services provider) have integrated economic informality into their distribution chains. Safaricom uses kiosks and sometimes hawkers to distribute its airtime credit cards. It also uses micro-retailers as agents for its monumental money transfer system, M-Pesa. Equity Bank (one of the major banks in Kenya, boasting 8 million customers) has cashed in on economic informality by situating its branches in dominant

118

economic informality spaces such as Gikomba, Kariobangi, Kawangware, Githurai, Kangemi and Ngara, to mention just a few. The fact that the formal sector is using principles of economic informality in its supply and distribution points illustrates the dynamism and special role that economic informality can play if it is given the same preferences that are awarded to formal firms.

### Women in the city

Although women were historically disadvantaged in society, the number of women in the city has increased. However, women have lower levels of education than men, making them more likely to turn to informality and live in informal settlements. There is also still a lack of female dominance in the city, although women have overcome great odds in the country's history to become shapers of the city landscape. In pre-independence and early post-independence times, there were no official policies to support women migrants. In 1968, parliament passed the Vagrancy and Prostitution Act, which allowed policemen to arrest indiscriminately women suspected of being prostitutes or vagrants. It was not until 1979 that women were issued with identity cards. The lack of identity cards had denied women the chance to transact business in banks or to own land. There was generally a negative attitude towards women migrants, and women who migrated as wives were generally under the control of their husbands. In patriarchal family settings, women had to seek permission from their husbands to secure employment or start a business. They could not even use their income freely as they were obliged to pool it within a family setting. A married woman without a job stayed in the city at her husband's discretion and he could decide to repatriate her back to the rural area at any time. The woman was therefore subordinated at both the household and the state level and confined to spaces with limited circuits of capital, power and commodities. Revitalizing their entrepreneurial acumen and responding to the high cost of living brought about by the structural adjustment programmes, women slowly surmounted existing barriers and stereotypes and plunged into the world of informal business. Their participation in economic informality is a struggle against material deprivation that has come about because of patriarchy and planning policies. One of the ways in which women reclaim themselves from material deprivation is through trade. These women's efforts are in line with Mikell's (1997) perspective on African feminism, which is concerned with the acquisition of basic needs.

Women's mobility is controlled in most traditional cultures. Lack of accessibility and free movement promotes subordination and the marginalization of people into informal settlements, whereas mobility helps overcome material deprivation. Through mobility, people acquire new ideas and exposure. Mobility provides women with independence and new openings and has enabled them to supplement family incomes, invest, offer social support, set up enterprises and educate their children, as well as buy homes. Thus, mobility to different spaces serves as a basis for women's transformation and liberation.

Women in economic informality are not a homogeneous category, as discussed in Chapter 6. They are drawn from many backgrounds in terms of age, education, marital status, location of their business, and source of working capital. Economic informality for women is a socio-cultural logic of managing poverty and creating employment as well as a way of achieving inclusion in the urbanism project. Since economic informality is not counted in government statistics, the role of women and their contribution to the national economy remain invisible. There is a need to see the possibility of a city constructed on a platform of economic informality, stable households and human capital.

Although city authorities have never been supportive of the informal sector and have worked to remove it from the central business district (CBD), women have used every opportunity to gain entry to the CBD (in areas such as Taveta Road). Employing Mr Nelson Kajuma's free market stalls concept, women have entered the city's CBD and are doing thriving business. Solidarity entrepreneurship based on the African indigenous market, whereby individuals use their collective self-belief to make investments and share transactions in collaboration with others, has played a critical role in the movement of women from the margins to the centre in their quest for spatial justice. By sharing and supporting each other, women are helping to reconfigure the city and construct feminine spaces through individual and solidarity entrepreneurship. By feminizing Kajuma's concept, women have brought the African indigenous market concept to the CBD and have contributed to the transformation of the city space.

## Implications for planning

This case study has highlighted the importance of informal businesses in the city and it calls for planners to appreciate the role of these businesses. It calls for the need to recognize the role of self-initiative in different groups in the city. The women studied in this book have navigated through discriminative policies and have used the feminine genius of mobility, entrepreneurialism and solidarity to move from the margins to the centre. This initiative, which was prompted by the desire to nurture their offspring or by the subaltern reason of livelihood negotiation, has contributed to the changing morphology of the CBD. This calls for city planners to study how different groups of people – as defined by demographics such as ethnicity, income, race, age and religion – shape the morphology of the city. City planners ought to learn from women and embrace the culture of nurturing and sustainability, as this will make policies people-centred and long term.

This case study has also shown that people in economic informality make the effort to legalize their businesses by acquiring permits. The business permit needs to be a more inclusive document that legitimizes economic informality in the city. The permit fee can include a form of taxation, which will ensure that people in economic informality contribute to the national income like all other citizens.

The city council should endeavour to develop infrastructure where economic informality operates – keep it clean and offer security. If the spaces of economic informality are not kept clean and secure, people feel alienated. This discourages them from being active participants in the city's welfare. By being denied access to infrastructure, the people in economic informality are not socialized into a culture of belonging to the city. Thus, they create their own institutions, such as *vyama*, to solve their problems. The city should incorporate these institutions that people have created or that they use to negotiate their livelihoods into some of its endeavours to manage the city.

Women have been unlearning the culture of poverty and becoming part of the solution by negotiating livelihoods through their *vyama*. The planners need to unlearn the culture of privilege in city hall that blinds them to the efforts of ordinary people in the management of everyday life. In the words of Miraftab (2009), the planners need to decolonize and de-westernize their planning perspectives so that they can incorporate some of the African forms and norms of livelihood negotiation and specialities, as was done by the first city government when it incorporated the first African indigenous market concept into the city. They also need to de-masculinize their planning strategy by introducing aspects of solidarity, including others and embracing norms of nurturing that have driven women into entrepreneurship.

This case study provides hope rather than the dystopia that is characteristic of literature on African cities. We need a paradigm shift in our perspectives on informality. We should not, as many researchers and academics do, view economic informality as the 'wounded' sector. The economic informality sector is full of possibilities. The discourse should move away from issues of insurgency, slumdog cities, grey cities and zones of exemption to analytical terms based on African norms such as ubuntu cities (cities of solidarity) and self-initiatives.

According to Kamete's (2012) perspective, this is the time to start interrogating the application of planning power in African cities. As this case study has shown, it is important for planners to come up with incentives for economic informality. Such inducements should include spatial justice incentives such as tax holidays, special zones, infrastructure, special parks, lease programmes, subsidies, and more space to set up businesses. This is the opportune time for planners to address the question of space in the city with regard to economic informality.

The case study is in agreement with Mikell's (1997) observation that the situation of women in African states and the problems they experience emanate from both patriarchal positions taken by men and decisions made by state leaders. In this case study, I demonstrated how the colonial and postcolonial governments,

121

in their desire to control male labour migrants, controlled women and denied them opportunities to move to the city. The post-independence government went a step further by introducing laws of vagrancy and prostitution that contributed to the marginalization of women in the city. On the other hand, the post-independence city administration treats women in the same way as it treats men, which means that it fails to appreciate the specific needs of women that accrue from their gender. In this light, it is important that city authorities also scrutinize their policies in terms of gender.

Although Kenya has adopted a new constitution that has opened up space for women, women's representation in the city government is still limited. There is a need to feminize the democratization process, not only in representation but also by introducing the norms of solidarity and nurturing. Programmes and projects in the city should not be driven only by the desire to maximize profits and cut costs; they should look into issues of solidarity, nurturing and protection.

The case study has shown the importance of mobility, accessibility and free movement for women and the implications these factors have on women's participation in economic informality. When planning for infrastructure, planners need to be aware of the importance of mobility because it contributes to women's ability to overcome material deprivation.

Planners also need to learn from below: that is, they should learn from the ordinary person, the subaltern. Planners should find out how ordinary citizens operate, their norms, values, aesthetics and institutions, and incorporate these lessons into theory and practice. Myers (2011) acknowledges this when he says that 'urban dwellers in Africa often develop their own forms and norms'.

This case study has illustrated how women have traversed policies in the city to acquire space and opportunity. This is a possibility that can be built upon to solve some of the urban problems in a large majority of cities. It can also serve as a basis for initiating dialogue between urban planners, authorities and the individuals engaged in economic informality.

Urban planners during the first decade of independence, faced with the challenge of implementing the ideals of self-governance as well as creating the foundations of an African city based on African norms of solidarity and equality, introduced the concept of the African indigenous market in the city. As a result of this strategy, economic informality in the city was institutionalized. Thus, while a large section of the literature depicts the unplanned nature of African cities, there is documented archival evidence that illustrates the planners' initiatives to plan the city. Today's planners need to learn from those of the first decade after independence and include economic informality in city master plans, development plans and national statistics.

While planners think of making Nairobi a world-class city, they should not do this at the expense of African culture. A visit to cities in the West and the Orient, for example, will reveal that they have an inbuilt cultural element. It is important that African cities be looked at in terms of their spatiality, ideas, resources and practices, such as the African indigenous market concept, solidarity entrepreneurialism, the inclusion of women in urban planning, and collective organization. Nairobi city should be seen through its complex history, culture and economy. It should also be understood through the way in which people have transformed it and how it has in turn changed them. City planners ought to give Nairobi city a cultural distinction that will make it stand out in the world. In doing this, they can use the example of economic informality businesswomen along Taveta Road, who have reconfigured the city by bringing the African indigenous market concept to the CBD. This market concept has been struggling to survive in cities in the context of the state's modernizing strategies that aim to introduce new forms of entrepreneurship, market transaction, accumulation and wealth distribution. However, this mode of business organization, which was previously confined to city council markets outside the CBD, has found its way into the centre of the city. It is embedding itself and changing the city landscape.

Another transformation that has taken place in the city is the entry of women to the CBD, where they are creating female spaces. Despite the fact that women were confined to the margins prior to Kenya's independence in 1963, they are gradually leaving the margins, moving to the CBD, and acquiring space there. This is an indication that people want to change their lives for the better, make the city conducive to economic informality and construct new spaces of action. To do so, they are borrowing from the past by introducing the African indigenous market concept into the city centre. The women are doing this through mobility, solidarity entrepreneurialism and collective organization.

As the World Bank enters into a partnership with the Nairobi county government to develop guidelines that will transform the Eastlands region, for example, into a sustainable city, local residents, including women and people in economic informality, need to be consulted. As illustrated in this case study, citizens have agency and can direct and configure change in their lives and environments. The fact that economic informality has persisted and weathered socioeconomic and political storms is an indicator that economic informality operators, as well as all other groups and movements in the city, should be included in the city planning process and in the creation of the Integrated Urban Development Master Plan for Nairobi.

# References

Abele, B. (1997) 'Over 150 women participate in women rights workshop'. *Daily
Nation*, 29 September.

Adichie, N. C. (2009) *Half of a Yellow Sun*.
New York NY: Harper Perennial.

Akinola, S. R. (2007) 'Coping with
infrastructural deprivation through
collective action among rural people in
Nigeria'. *Nordic Journal of African Studies*
16(1): 30–46.

Anyona, S. (1996) 'Culture, not law better
protection of women's rights'. *Daily
Nation*, 10 August.

Bangura, Y. (1994) 'Economic restructuring, coping strategies and social
change: implications for institutional
development in Africa'. *Development
and Change* 25(4): 785–827. http://
dx.doi.org/10.1111/j.1467-7660.1994.
tb00536.x.

Barnes, T. A. (1992) 'The fight for control of African women's mobility
in colonial Zimbabwe, 1900–1939'.
*Signs* 17(3): 586–608. http://dx.doi.
org/10.1086/494750.

Basu, A. (1995) 'Introduction'. In A. Basu
(ed.) *The Challenge of Local Feminisms:
Women's movements in global perspective*,
pp. 1–21. Boulder CO: Westview Press.

Bayart, J. F. (1999) '"The social capital" of
the felonious state'. In J. F. Bayart,
S. Ellis and B. Hibou (eds) *The Criminal-
ization of the State in Africa*, pp. 32–48.
Oxford: James Currey.

Bayat, A. (2000) 'From "dangerous classes"
to "quiet rebels": politics of the
urban subalterns in the global
south'. *International Sociology*
15(3): 533–57. http://dx.doi.org/
10.1177/026858000015003005.

Beall, J., B. Guha-Khasnobis and
R. Kanbur (2010) 'Introduction: African
development in an urban world: beyond the tipping point'. *Urban Forum* 21
(3): 187–204. http://dx.doi.org/10.1007/
s12132-010-9086-5.

Beoku-Betts, J. and W. N. Njambi (2005)
'African feminist scholars in women's
studies: negotiating spaces of dislocation and transformation in the study
of women'. *Meridians: Feminism, Race,
Transnationalism* 6(1): 113–32.

Berrou, J.-P. and F. Combarnous (2012)
'The personal networks of entrepreneurs in an informal African urban
economy: does the "strength of ties"
matter?' *Review of Social Economy* 70(1):
1–30.

Bett, A. C. (1967) 'Women are equals'. *Daily
Nation*, 19 December.

Boserup, E. (1970) *Women's Role in Economic
Development*. London: Earthscan.

Bourdieu, P. (1986) 'The forms of capital'.
In J. G. Richardson (ed.) *Handbook of
Theory and Research for the Sociology of
Education*, pp. 241–58. New York NY:
Greenwood Press.

Bromley, R. (1978) 'Introduction – the
urban informal sector: why is it worth
discussing?' *World Development* 6(9–10):
1033–9. http://dx.doi.org/10.1016/0305-
750X(78)90061-X.

Brown, A. (2006) *Contested Space: Street
trading, public space, and livelihoods in
developing cities*. Rugby: Practical Action Publishing.

Bueuret, K. (1991) 'Women and Transport'. In M. McLean and D. Grove (eds) *Women's Issues in Social Policy*, pp. 61–75. London: Routledge.

Bujra, J. M. (1975) 'Women "entrepreneurs" of early Nairobi'. *Canadian Journal of African Studies* 9(2): 213–34. http://dx.doi.org/10.2307/484081.

Büscher, M. and J. Urry (2009) 'Mobile methods and the empirical'. *European Journal of Social Theory* 12(1): 99–116. http://dx.doi.org/10.1177/1368431008099642.

Cass, N., E. Shove and J. Urry (2005) 'Social exclusion, mobility and access'. *The Sociological Review* 53(3): 539–55. http://dx.doi.org/10.1111/j.1467-954X.2005.00565.x.

Chabal, P. and J. P. Daloz (1999) *Africa Works: Disorder as political instrument*. Oxford and Bloomington IN: International African Institute with James Currey and Indiana University Press.

Chant, S. (2013) 'Cities through a "gender lens": a golden "urban age" for women in the global south?' *Environment and Urbanization* 25(1): 9–29. http://dx.doi.org/10.1177/0956247813477809.

Chant, S. and C. Pedwell (2008) *Women, Gender and the Informal Economy: An assessment of ILO research and suggested ways forward*. Geneva: International Labour Organization (ILO).

Chen, A. (2007) 'Rethinking the informal economy: linkages with the formal economy and the formal regulatory environment'. DESA Working Paper No. 46, pp. 1–46. New York NY: United Nations Department of Economic and Social Affairs (DESA).

Chen, A. M., J. Vanek and M. Carr (2004) *Mainstreaming Informal Employment and Gender in Poverty Reduction: A handbook for policy-makers and other stakeholders*. London: Commonwealth Secretariat.

Clark, G. (2010) 'Gender fictions and gender tensions involving "traditional" Asante market women'. *African Studies Quarterly* 11(2&3): 43–66.

COHRE (2008) *Women, Slums and Urbanisation: Examining the causes and consequences*. Geneva: Centre on Housing Rights and Evictions (COHRE), Women and Housing Rights Programme.

Coleman, J. S. (1988) 'Social capital in the creation of human capital'. *American Journal of Sociology* 94(s1 Suppl.): S95–120. http://dx.doi.org/10.1086/228943.

Crane, R. and L. Takahashi (2009) 'Sex changes everything: the recent narrowing and widening of travel differences by gender'. *Public Works Management and Policy* 13(4): 328–37. http://dx.doi.org/10.1177/1087724X09335608.

Dahal, G. R. and K. P. Adhikari (2008) 'Bridging, linking and bonding social capital in collective action'. CAPRi Working Paper No. 79. Washington DC: Systemwide Program on Collective Action and Property Rights (CAPRi).

*Daily Nation* (1966) 'City council to advertise market stalls'. 19 December.

*Daily Nation* (1967a) 'Markets' new look'. 14 January.

*Daily Nation* (1967b) 'Prostitutes will be repatriated under bill'. 21 November.

*Daily Nation* (1974) 'Illegal kiosks'. 30 May.

*Daily Nation* (1980) 'A brighter life for kiosks'. 7 March.

*Daily Nation* (1981) 'Council warns on illegal kiosks'. 19 March.

*Daily Nation* (1987) 'Hawker issue sparks debate in city meeting'. 20 June.

*Daily Nation* (1989) 'Clearing Nairobi undesirables'. 9 February.

*Daily Nation* (1990a) 'Mungai criticizes Gumo over kiosks'. 31 March.

*Daily Nation* (1990b) 'Muoroto commission boss parades askaris'. 13 June.

*Daily Nation* (1990c) 'No to hucksters of street violence'. 28 September.

*Daily Nation* (1996) 'Women most hit by SAPs'. 13 February.

*Daily Nation* (1998a) 'Hawkers eviction to go on'. 24 April.

*Daily Nation* (1998b) 'Traders, police battle it out'. 1 May.

*Daily Nation* (2002) 'Control hawking business'. 31 July.

*Daily Nation* (2006a) 'Hawkers to exit town centre'. 15 July.

*Daily Nation* (2006b) 'Ministries blamed for menace by city hawkers'. 21 October.

Davis, M. (2004) 'Planet of slums: urban involution and the informal proletariat'. *New Left Review* 26:5–34.

de Olarte, E. G. (2001) 'Hernando de Soto's mysteries'. *SAIS Review of International Affairs* 21(1): 275–82.

de Soto, H. (1989) *The Other Path: The economic answer to terrorism*. New York NY: Basic Books.

Deininger, K. (2003) *Land Policies for Growth and Poverty Reduction*. World Bank Policy Research Report. Washington DC: World Bank.

Diallo, A. (2003) 'Paradoxes of female sexuality in Mali: on the practices of *Magnonmaka* and *Bolokoli-kela*'. In S. Amfred (ed.) *Rethinking Sexualities in Africa*, pp. 173–94. Uppsala: Nordic African Institute.

Donaldson, S. R. (1997) '"Our women keep our skies from falling": women's networks and survival imperatives in Tshunyane, South Africa'. In G. Mikell (ed.) *African Feminism: The politics of survival in sub-Saharan Africa*, pp. 257–75.
Philadelphia PA: University of Pennsylvania Press.

Easterly, W. (2005) 'What did structural adjustments adjust? The association of policies and growth with repeated IMF and World Bank adjustment loans'. *Journal of Development Economics* 76(1): 1–22. http://dx.doi.org/10.1016/S0304-3878(04)00087-2.

Fapohunda, M. T. (2012) 'Women and the informal sector in Nigeria: implications for development'. *British Journal of Arts and Social Sciences* 4(1): 35–45.

Freund, B. (2007) *The African City: A history*. Cambridge: Cambridge University Press.

Gacheri, J. R. (1995) 'Women see the light at the end of the dark tunnel'. *Daily Nation*, 1 May.

Garland, A. M., M. Massoumi and B. A. Ruble (2007) *Global Urban Poverty: Setting the agenda*. Washington DC: Woodrow Wilson International Center for Scholars.

Graham, S. and S. Marvin (2001) *Splintering Urbanism: Networked infrastructures, technological mobilities and the urban condition*. London: Routledge. http://dx.doi.org/10.4324/9780203452202.

Hanson, S. (2010) 'Gender and mobility: new approaches for informing sustainability'. *Gender, Place and Culture* 17(1): 5–23. http://dx.doi.org/10.1080/09663690903498225.

Harris, N. (1992) *Cities in the 1990s: The challenge for countries*. London: University College London.

Hart, K. (1973) 'Informal income opportunities and urban employment in Ghana'. *Journal of Modern African Studies* 11(1): 61–89. http://dx.doi.org/10.1017/S0022278X00008089.

Hlela, K. S. (2003) 'Dilemmas of collective action in the informal economy: how the other quarter lives?' *Policy: Issues and Actors* 16(4): 1–19.

Hyden, G. (1983) *No Shortcut to Progress: African development management in perspective*. London: Heinemann.

ILO (1972) *Employment, Incomes and Equality: A strategy for increasing productive employment in Kenya*. Geneva: International Labour Organization (ILO).

ILO (2002) *Women and Men in the Informal Economy: A statistical picture*. Geneva: International Labour Organization (ILO).

Jennings, M. (1994) 'Gender issues in the informal sector: constraints and opportunities'. In *Trócaire Development Review 1993–94*, pp. 49–66. Maynooth, Ireland: Trócaire.

Jirón, P. (2010) 'Mobile borders in urban daily mobility practices in Santiago de Chile'. *International Political Sociology* 4(1): 66–79. http://dx.doi.org/10.1111/j.1749-5687.2009.00092.x.

Kamete, A. Y. (2012) 'Interrogating planning's power in an African city: time for reorientation?' *Planning Theory* 11(1): 66–88. http://dx.doi.org/10.1177/1473095211419116.

Kamete, A. Y. (2013a) 'On handling urban informality in Southern Africa'. *Geografiska Annaler* 95(1): 17–31. http://dx.doi.org/10.1111/geob.12007.

Kamete, A. Y. (2013b) 'Missing the point? Urban planning and the normalisation of "pathological" spaces in southern Africa'. *Transactions of the Institute of British Geographers* 38(4): 639–51. http://dx.doi.org/10.1111/j.1475-5661.2012.00552.x.

Kamunyori, W. (2007) 'A growing space for dialogue: the case of street vending in Nairobi's central business district'. Unpublished MA thesis, Department of Urban Studies and Planning, Massachusetts Institute of Technology.

Karanja, M. A. (1996) 'Entrepreneurship among rural women in Kenya'. In D. McCormick and O. P. Pedersen (eds) *Small Enterprises: Flexibility and networking in an African context*, pp. 131–42. Nairobi: Longhorn Kenya.

Kebede, W. and A. K. Butterfield (2009) 'Social networks among poor women in Ethiopia'. *International Social Work* 52(3): 357–73. http://dx.doi.org/10.1177/0020872808102069.

Kenya National Archives (1937–63) Hawkers by-laws. RN/8/4.

Kenya National Archives (1950) *A Jubilee History 1900–1950*. MSS 115/20/32.

Kenya National Archives (1962) City council document 6/9/12.

Kenya National Archives (1964) Correspondence of women dignitaries. Minutes of council of women of Kenya about home industries. MSS/57/29.

Kenya National Archives (1964–78) Hawkers by-laws. JA/15/5.

Kenya National Archives (1965a) Memo from town clerk to the permanent secretary ministry of local government. RN/1/169.

Kenya National Archives (1965b) Kenya Council of Women. International correspondence 1961–66. MSS/57/31.

Kenya National Archives (1972a) Letter to President Mzee Jomo Kenyatta by Kenya Street Traders Society on hawkers problems in Nairobi and the solution. RN/1/169.

Kenya National Archives (1972b) Memo from market superintendent to the town clerk on hawker licences. RN/1/169.

Kenya National Archives (1973a) City council of Nairobi: conferences and congress. RN/2/1/3.

Kenya National Archives (1973b) Memo from licensing superintendent to the town clerk on hawker licences. RN/1/169.

Kenya National Archives (1974) Conference on hawkers and vendors organized by development research centre in collaboration with the Asian Institute of Management in the Philippines: Nairobi case study by J. P. Mbogua. RN/1/169.

Kenya National Archives (1975a) Hon. Mwangi Mathei's (MP Langata Constituency) letter to Miss Margaret Kenyatta on hawker licences. RN/1/1969.

Kenya National Archives (1975b) Letter to the town clerk by a hawker on *irio* and *ugali* kiosk. RN/1/169.

Kenya National Archives (1976) Report on the proposed construction of hawkers' kiosks phase 1. JA/15/5.

Kenya National Archives (1978) Memo from licensing superintendent to the town clerk on licensing of city council markets. RN/1/170.

Khayesi, M., H. Monheim and J. M. Nebe (2010) 'Negotiating "streets for all" in urban transport planning: the case for pedestrians, cyclists and street vendors in Nairobi, Kenya'. *Antipode* 42(1): 103–26. http://dx.doi.org/10.1111/j.1467-8330.2009.00733.x.

Kinyanjui, M. N. (1999) 'The search for a gender-sensitive development policy'. In N. Ng'ethe and W. Owino (eds) *From Sessional Paper No. 10 of 1965 to Structural Adjustment: Towards indigenizing the policy debates*, pp. 267–300. Nairobi: Institute of Policy Analysis and Research (IPAR).

Kinyanjui, M. N. (2003) 'A gender analysis of small scale garment producers' response to market liberalisation in Kenya'. *African Geographical Review* 22(1): 49–59.

Kinyanjui, M. N. (2008a) 'From home to *jua kali* enterprise spaces: entrepreneurship and gender identity'. *Journal of Small Business and Entrepreneurship* 5(3/4): 401–11.

Kinyanjui, M. N. (2008b) 'Is informal enterprise a path to urban socio-economic dynamism in Nairobi?' IDS Working Paper No. 4. Milton Keynes: International Development Centre (IDS).

Kinyanjui, M. N. (2010) *Social Relations and Associations in the Informal Sector in Kenya*. UNRISD Social Policy and Development Paper No. 43. Geneva: United Nations Research Institute for Social Development (UNRISD).

Kinyanjui, M. N. (2011) '*Jua kali* strategies for socio-economic change in Nairobi'. *Hemispheres: Studies on Cultures and Societies* 26: 29–46.

Kinyanjui, M. N. (2012) *Institutions of Hope: Ordinary people's market coordination and society organisation alternatives*. Nairobi: Nsemia Publishers.

Kinyanjui, M. N. (2013) 'Women informal garment traders in Taveta Road, Nairobi: from the margins to the center'. *African Studies Review* 56 (3): 147–64. http://dx.doi.org/10.1017/asr.2013.83.

Kinyanjui, M. N. and W. Gichuhi (2010) '*Kamweretho*: politics from below on motherhood in a developmental context'. Paper presented at the Pan African Conference on Strengths of the African Family, Mombasa, 14–19 August.

Kraus, J. (1991) 'The struggle over structural adjustment in Ghana'. *Africa Today* 38 (4): 19–37.

Lang, J. (1992) 'Women and transport'. *Urban Transport* 10: 14–24.

Larsen, L., S. L. Harlan, B. Bolin, E. J. Hackett, D. Hope, A. Kirby, A. Nelson, T. R. Rex and S. Wolf (2004) 'Bonding and bridging: understanding the relationship between social capital and civic action'. *Journal of Planning Education and Research* 24(1): 64–77. http://dx.doi.org/10.1177/0739456X04267181.

Larson, J. E. (2002) 'Informality, illegality, and inequality'. *Yale Law & Policy Review* 20(1): 137–82.

Law, R. (1999) 'Beyond "women and transport": towards new geographies of gender and daily mobility'. *Progress in Human Geography* 23(4): 567–88. http://dx.doi.org/10.1191/030913299666161864.

Lazar, S. (2007) 'In-between and the margins: collective organisation, ethnicity and political agency among Bolivian street traders'. In J. Staples (ed.) *Livelihoods and the Margins: Surviving the city*, pp. 237–56. Walnut Creek CA: Left Coast Press.

Lindell, I. (2010a) 'Between exit and voice: informality and the spaces for popular agency'. *African Studies Quarterly* 11(2&3): 1–8.

Lindell, I. (2010b) 'Introduction: the changing politics of informality – collective organizing, alliances and scales of engagement'. In I. Lindell (ed.) *Africa's Informal Workers: Collective agency, alliances and transnational organizing in urban Africa*, pp. 1–30. London: Zed Books.

Little, J. (1994) *Gender, Planning and the Policy Process*. Oxford: Pergamon Press.

Mabogunje, A. L. (1968) *Urbanization in Nigeria*. London: University of London Press.

Mabogunje, A. L. (1984) 'Backwash urbanization: the peasantization of cities in sub-Saharan Africa'. In M. P. Conzen (ed.) *World Patterns of Modern Urban Change: Essays in honor of Chauncey D. Harris*, pp. 255–72. Chicago IL: University of Chicago Press.

Macharia, K. (1997) *Social and Political Dynamics of the Informal Economy in African Cities: Nairobi and Harare*. Lanham MD: University Press of America.

Macharia, K. (2003) 'Migration in Kenya and its impacts on the labor market'. Paper prepared for the conference on African Migration in Comparative Perspectives, Johannesburg, 4–7 June.

Maina-Ahlberg, B. (1991) *Women, Sexuality and the Changing Social Order: The impact of government policies on reproductive behavior in Kenya*. Amsterdam: Gordon and Breach Science Publishers.

Maloney, W. F. (1999) 'Does informality imply segmentation in urban labour markets? Evidence from sectoral transitions in Mexico'. *World Bank Economic Review* 13(2): 275–302. http://dx.doi.org/10.1093/wber/13.2.275.

Mandel, J. L. (2004) 'Mobility matters: women's livelihood strategies in Porto Novo, Benin'. *Gender, Place and Culture* 11(2): 257–87. http://dx.doi.org/10.1080/0966369042000218482.

Mathiu, M. (1998) 'Women's day'. *Sunday Nation*, 8 March.

Mbembe, J. A. and S. Nutall (2004) 'Writing the world from an African metropolis'. *Public Culture* 16(3): 347–72. http://dx.doi.org/10.1215/08992363-16-3-347.

Mbiti, J. S. (1969) *African Religions and Philosophy*. Nairobi: Heinemann Kenya.

McCall, D. T. (1955) 'Dynamics of urbanization in Africa'. *Annals of the American Academy of Political and Social Science* 298(1): 151–60. http://dx.doi.org/10.1177/000271625529800116.

McCormick, D. (1999) 'African enterprise clusters and industrialization: theory and reality'. *World Development* 27(9): 1531–51. http://dx.doi.org/10.1016/S0305-750X(99)00074-1.

McCormick, D., W. V. Mitullah and M. Kinyanjui (2003) 'How to collaborate: associations and other community-based organizations among Kenyan micro and small-scale entrepreneurs'. IDS Occasional Paper No. 70. Milton Keynes: Institute for Development Studies (IDS).

Meagher, K. (2010) *Identity Economics: Social networks and the informal economy in Nigeria*. Woodbridge: James Currey.

Meagher, K. (2011) 'Informal economies and urban governance in Nigeria: popular empowerment or political exclusion?' *African Studies Review* 54 (2): 47–72. http://dx.doi.org/10.1353/arw.2011.0026.

Meagher, K. (2012) 'Weber meets Godzilla: social networks and the spirit of capitalism in East Asia and Africa'. *Review of African Political Economy* 39(132): 261–78. http://dx.doi.org/10.1080/03056244.2012.688804.

Mikell, G. (1997) *African Feminism: The politics of survival in sub-Saharan Africa*. Philadelphia PA: University of Pennsylvania Press.

Miraftab, F. (2009) 'Insurgent planning: situating radical planning in the global south'. *Planning Theory* 8(1): 32–50. http://dx.doi.org/10.1177/1473095208099297.

Mitullah, W. (2003) 'Street trade in Kenya: the contribution of research in policy dialogue and response'. Paper prepared for the Urban Research Symposium on Urban Development for Economic Growth and Poverty Reduction, World Bank, Washington, 15–17 December.

Mitullah, W. (2007) 'Street vendors and informal trading: the struggle for the right to trade'. In F. Manji and P. Burnett (eds) *From the Slave Trade to 'Free' Trade: How trade undermines democracy and justice in Africa*, pp. 119–24. Oxford: Fahamu Books.

Mohanty, C. T. (1988) 'Under western eyes: feminist scholarship and colonial discourses'. *Feminist Review* 30: 61–88.

Moser, C. (1978) 'Informal sector or petty commodity production: dualism or dependency in urban development?' *World Development* 6(9–10): 1041–64. http://dx.doi.org/10.1016/0305-750X(78)90062-1.

Moser, C. and J. Holland (1997) *Household Responses to Poverty and Vulnerability. Vol. 4: Confronting crisis in Chawama, Lusaka, Zambia*. Washington DC: World Bank, Urban Management Programme.

Mugo, G. M. (2012) *Writing and Speaking from the Heart of My Mind: Selected essays and speeches*. Trenton NJ: African World Press.

Muhavi, D. J. (1969) 'Young wives'. *Saturday Nation*, 22 February.

Muiruri, P. (2010) Women Street Vendors in Nairobi, Kenya: A situational and policy analysis within a human rights framework. Addis Ababa: Organization for Social Science Research in Eastern and Southern Africa.

Mulwa, M. (2009) 'Why form squad to fight the poor'. *Daily Nation*, 3 June.

Munene, F. (1972) 'Pregnant girls need social care: not social isolation'. *Daily Nation*, 15 December.

Murray, M. J. and G. A. Myers (2006) *Cities in Contemporary Africa*. New York NY: Palgrave Macmillan.

Mutongi, B. K. (2006) 'Thugs or entrepreneurs? Perceptions of *matatu* operators in Nairobi, 1970 to the present'. *Africa: Journal of the International Africa Institute* 76(4): 549–68. http://dx.doi.org/10.3366/afr.2006.0072.

Mwakisha, J. (1991) 'Different focus'. *Daily Nation*, 8 March.

Mwangi, K. (1990) 'City askaris invade Gikomba'. *Daily Nation*, 6 July.

Myers, G. (2011) *African Cities: Alternative visions of urban theory and practice*. London: Zed Books.

Ndii, D. (1998) 'Gender sensitivity and gravy train'. *Sunday Nation*, 18 October.

Ng'alwa, N. B. (1970) 'Too many women in jobs'. *Sunday Nation*, 10 March.

Ngau, M. P. and I. C. Keino (1996) 'Women's social background and entrepreneurship in Nairobi'. In D. McCormick and P. O. Pedersen (eds) *Small Enterprises: Flexibility and networking in an African context*, pp. 113–30. Nairobi: Longhorn Kenya.

Ngwala, T. A. (2011) 'Planning development challenges of micro retail/shops in Luthuli Avenue of the central business district of Nairobi'. Unpublished BA planning research project, University of Nairobi.

Ngwiri, A. (1998) 'Seminars yes, but women need more'. *Daily Nation*, 3 August.

Nijman, J. (2010) 'A study of space in Mumbai's slums'. *Tijdschrift voor Economische en Sociale Geografie* 101(1): 4–17. http://dx.doi.org/10.1111/j.1467-9663.2009.00576.x.

Njihia, G. (1985) 'No easy solution to the issue of hawkers'. *Daily Nation*, 13 September.

Nnaemeka, O. (2003) 'Nego-feminism: theorizing, practicing, and pruning Africa's way'. Signs: *Journal of Women in Culture and Society* 29(2): 358–85.

Nte, N. D. (2010) 'The urban informal sector and workplace insecurity for women in Nigeria: evidence from Port Harcourt City'. *Bangladesh e-journal of Sociology* 7(2): 16–33.

Oduol, W. and M. W. Kabira (1995) 'The mother of warriors and her daughters: the women's movement in Kenya'. In A. Basu (ed.) *The Challenge of Local Feminisms: Women's movements in global perspective*, pp. 87–208. Boulder CO: Westview Press.

Okuro, S. O. (2006) 'Misfit mothers, wayward wives and disobedient daughters'. *Les Cahiers d'Afrique de l'Est* 31: 39–81.

Olchurie, C. E. (1966) 'Women of Kenya are on our way'. *Daily Nation*, 22 April.

Onyango, P. (2010) *Cultural Gap and Economic Crisis in Africa: Africa must reinvent herself in order to overcome her economic crisis. Focus on the sub-Saharan region*. Peterborough: FastPrint Publishing.

Opanga, K. (1989) 'Court ruling highlights street hawkers' rights'. *Daily Nation*, 11 October.

Ostrom, E. (1990) *Governing the Commons: The evolution of institutions for collective action*. Cambridge: Cambridge University Press. http://dx.doi.org/10.1017/CBO9780511807763.

Oxfam (2012) *Women's Collective Action: Unlocking the potential of agricultural markets*. Oxford: Oxfam International. Available at www.womenscollectiveaction.com.

Pattison, K. (1975) 'Maridadi Fabrics: where deserted and widowed are supported'. *Daily Nation*, 4 November.

Potts, D. (1995) 'Shall we go home? Increasing urban poverty in African cities and migration processes'. *Geographical*

*Journal* 161 (3): 245–64. http://dx.doi.org/10.2307/3059830.

Robertson, C. C. (1996) 'Transitions in Kenyan patriarchy: attempts to control Nairobi area traders, 1920–1963'. In K. Sheldon (ed.) *Courtyards, Markets, City Streets: Urban women in Africa*, pp. 31–46. Boulder CO: Westview Press.

Robertson, C. C. (1997) *Trouble Showed the Way: Women, men and trade in the Nairobi area, 1890–1990*. Bloomington IN: Indiana University Press.

Robinson, J. (2002) 'Global and world cities: a view from off the map'. *International Journal of Urban and Regional Research* 26(3): 531–54. http://dx.doi.org/10.1111/1468-2427.00397.

Robinson, J. (2006) *Ordinary Cities: Between modernity and development*. Abingdon: Routledge.

Roy, A. (2005) 'Urban informality: towards an epistemology of planning'. *Journal of the American Planning Association* 71(2): 147–58. http://dx.doi.org/10.1080/01944360508976689.

Roy, A. (2009) 'Why India cannot plan its cities: informality, insurgence and the idiom of urbanization'. *Planning Theory* 8(76): 77–87.

Roy, A. (2011) 'Slumdog cities: rethinking subaltern urbanisms'. *International Journal of Urban and Regional Research* 35(2): 223–38.

Schlyter, A. (2009) 'Body politics and the crafting of citizenship in peri-urban Lusaka'. *Feminist Africa* 13: 23–43.

Schmitz, H. and K. Nadvi (1999) 'Clustering and industrialization: introduction'. *World Development* 27(9): 1503–14. http://dx.doi.org/10.1016/S0305-750X(99)00072-8.

Sheldon, K. (1996) 'Urban African women: courtyards, markets, city streets'. In K. Sheldon (ed.) *Courtyards, Markets, City Streets: Urban women in Africa*, pp. 3–30. Boulder CO: Westview Press.

Sheller, M. (2004) 'Mobile publics: beyond the network perspective'. *Environment and Planning D: Society and Space* 22(1): 39–52. http://dx.doi.org/10.1068/d324t.

Simone, A. (2001a) 'Straddling the divide: remaking associational life in the informal African city'. *International Journal of Urban and Regional Research* 25(1): 102–17. http://dx.doi.org/10.1111/1468-2427.00300.

Simone, A. (2001b) 'On the worlding of African cities'. *African Studies Review* 44 (2): 15–41. http://dx.doi.org/10.2307/525573.

Simone, A. (2004) 'People as infrastructures: intersecting fragments in Johannesburg'. *Public Culture* 16(3): 407–29. http://dx.doi.org/10.1215/08992363-16-3-407.

Simone, A. (2010) *The Social Infrastructures of City Life in Contemporary Africa*. Uppsala: Nordic Africa Institute.

Simone, A. (2011) 'The politics of urban intersection: materials, affect, bodies'. In G. Bridge and S. Watson (eds) The New Blackwell Companion to the City, pp. 357–66. Oxford: Blackwell.

Skinner, C. (2008) 'Women in informal employment; globalizing and organizing'. *Nordic Journal of African Studies* 16(1): 30–46.

Smart, J. (1950) *Nairobi: A jubilee history 1900–1950*. Nairobi: East African Standard.

Spivak, G. C. (1988) 'Can the subalterns speak?' In C. Nelson and L. Grossberg (eds) *Marxism and the Interpretation of Culture*, pp. 271–316. Champaign IL: University of Illinois Press.

Stamp, P. (1986) 'Kikuyu women self-help groups: towards an understanding of the relationship between sex-gender system and mode of production in Africa'. In C. Robertson and I. Berger (eds) *Women and Class in Africa*, pp. 27–46. New York NY: Holmes and Meier.

Sundberg, J. (2004) 'Identities in the making: conservation, gender and race in the Maya Biosphere Reserve, Guatemala'. *Gender, Place and Culture* 11(1): 43–66. http://dx.doi.org/10.1080/0966369042000188549.

Thorbek, S. (1988) 'Women and urbanization'. *Acta Sociologica* 31(4):

283–301. http://dx.doi.org/ 10.1177/000169938803100401.

Tsikata, D. (2009) 'Informalization, the informal economy and urban women's livelihoods in sub-Saharan Africa since the 1990s'. In S. Razavi (ed.) *The Gendered Impacts of Liberalization: Towards 'embedded liberalism'?*, pp. 131–62. New York NY and Abingdon: Routledge.

Turshen, M. (2010) 'The political economy of Women in Africa'. In M. Turshen (ed.) *African Women: A political economy*, pp. 1–22. New York NY: Palgrave Macmillan.

UN-HABITAT (2006) *Nairobi Urban Sector Profile*. Nairobi: United Nations Human Settlements Programme (UN-HABITAT).

Unni, J. (2001) 'Gender and informality in labour markets in Asia'. *Economic and Political Weekly* 36(26): 2360–77.

Watson, V. (2002) 'The usefulness of normative planning theories in the context of sub-Saharan Africa'. *Planning Theory* 1(1): 27–52. http://dx.doi. org/10.1177/147309520200100103.

Watson, V. (2009) 'Seeing from the south: refocusing urban planning on the globe's central urban issues'. *Urban Studies* 46(11): 2259–75. http://dx.doi. org/10.1177/0042098009342598.

White, L. (1990) *The Comforts of Home: Prostitution in colonial Nairobi*. Chicago IL: University of Chicago Press. http://dx.doi.org/10.7208/chica go/9780226895000.001.0001.

Yiftachel, O. (2009) 'Critical theory and "gray space": mobilization of the colonized'. *City* 13(2–3): 246–63.

# Index

Note: *t* attached to a page number denotes a table

4, 87; and urban dystopia, 4; and urban planning, 5, 6–7, 22, 31
Combarnous, F., 101
council *see* city council
crime, 37, 41–2, 115
cultural diversity, 17–18
culture, 21, 108; *see also* music

de Soto, Hernando, 10, 14, 36, 87, 110
Diallo, A, 54
Donaldson, S. R., 101
donors, 13, 28

Eastlands, 28, 87, 123
economic informality *see* informal economy
education: by gender in Nairobi, 44–5, 44$t$; for girls, 60; lack of free school places, 53; school fees, 81–2, 85; of women in economic informality, 79; women's investment in, 84–6
elite women, 60–62
Ellis, George, 20
employment: advantages for women, 68–70; by women in informal economy, 81; city council attitude, 12; hostility towards women workers, 51–2; low-wage jobs, 21, 46
empowerment: financial, 68–70, 80–81; from *chama* membership, 107, 107$t$; political, 59–60, 114
entrepreneurship, 13, 14–15, 78, 82–3, 95–8
Equity Bank, 9, 92, 95, 118–19
ethnic segregation, 4, 31, 87, 117
evictions, 26, 38–40, 45

family: male breadwinner paradigm, 83–4; power relationships, 86; *see also* marriage; single motherhood
Family Bank, 92, 94
Fapohunda, M. T., 76
feminism, 53–5, 84, 119
finance: bank loans, 91–2, 94–5; *chama* membership, 105–7, 107$t$, 113, 114, 115; microfinance, 68, 68$t$, 80–81, 96; start-up capital, 67–8, 68$t$; for women's businesses, 80–81; women's household expenditure, 81–2
financial independence, 68–9
Fort Smith, 19

Forum for African Women Educationists, 60
free market stalls, 42, 91, 120
Freund, B., 4, 17
funerals, 31

Gachukia, Edda, 59–60
gangs, 41, 100
gender inequality, 7–8
Githunguri, G. G. J., 38
greengrocers (*mama mboga*), 2, 17, 62
Guatamala, women's mobility, 66
Gumo, Fred, 39–40

handicrafts, 58–9
Harare, Operation Restore Order, 6
Harris, N., 3
Hart, K., 8–9, 76, 77
hawkers: accused of criminal activity, 37–8; activities, 23, 24$t$, 25; agency, 30; association, 26; conflicts, 26–7, 33–4; early development of, 12; evictions, 26, 38–40, 45; harassment, 48, 61, 118; lack of security of tenure, 33–5; licenses for women, 48; licensing arrangements, 7, 12, 23–8, 38–40; premises, 80, 88$t$, 88–9; reasons for increase in, 40–41; relations with government, 40, 118; sanitation and cleanliness issues, 12, 26, 27, 34, 39; statistics, 24$t$, 25; unfair competition accusations, 38, 39; unlicensed, 26, 34, 38; *see also* indigenous (open-air) markets
home industries, 57–9
household expenditure, by women, 81–2
housing: for Africans, 21, 47; diversity, 18; interior design, 111; location of residences, 67, 67$t$; property ownership, 89
human capital, 84–7; *see also* education
human rights, 72–3

identity cards, 47, 51, 119
IMF, structural adjustment programmes, 13, 37, 52, 118
India, problems of informality, 5–6
indigenous (open-air) markets, 28–9, 32, 88$t$, 88–9, 118, 122; *see also* hawkers
informal economy: business premises, 80, 88$t$, 88–9; city revenue from, 114; definitions, 8, 14–15; dualist approach, 8–9; and employment of labour, 81; extent